Advance Praise for *The Trance of Scarcity*

"Victoria Castle's book is a brilliant journey into the trance that holds us captive and robs us of our sense of wholeness. The message of *The Trance of Scarcity* is vital to our time and creates the possibility for a kind of liberation that can have impact on all parts of one's life. I recommend this book to anyone and every."
—**Lynne Twist**, author of *The Soul of Money*

"It takes great effort to wake anybody out of a trance. Victoria's book does just that. This is an instructive, encouraging, and delightful book that I believe can wake us out of our numbed state, where we've forgotten our true nature, our fundamental human goodness. Please read it."
—**Margaret J. Wheatley**, author of *Leadership and the New Science* and *Finding Our Way: Leadership for an Uncertain Time*

"Of the two dimensions to our money issues—the inner and the outer—Victoria Castle is dealing with the inner side in a masterful way. I recommend this book to anybody who feels that money is a concern in their lives."
—**Bernard Lietaer**, author of *The Future of Money*

"Personal change can be very heady. Exhilarating, to be sure . . . but often disconnected from what the body knows. Your head can get you high, but it can also let you down. Mind and body together, though, help you steer your life truly. Victoria Castle gives you practices that foster body/mind collaboration to help you address *not-enough-ness* and successfully navigate change."
—**Vicki Robin**, co-author of *Your Money or Your Life*, co-founder *Conversation Cafés*

"In this insightful, accessible, and graceful book, Victoria Castle explains how Somatics can help free us from the stories of lack that imprison our thinking, emotions, perceptions, and vitality. Readers will appreciate the directness and simplicity of this compassionate, effective perspective for confronting a myth that has lived within us for centuries."
—**Richard Strozzi-Heckler, PhD**, Founder, Somatic Coaching, author of *In Search of the Warrior Spirit* and *The Anatomy of Change*

"Victoria Castle calls us all to awaken from our trance, see current reality with deeper clarity and courage, and realize the boundlessness of our true nature and highest human potential."
—**Dr. Joel & Michelle Levey**, authors of *Living in Balance* and *Wisdom at Work: The Fine Arts of Relaxation, Concentration, & Meditation*, founders of WisdomAtWork.com and the International Center for Corporate Culture & Organizational Health

"It is difficult to know how a false belief has held you captive, until you break free from it. Victoria Castle reveals how we literally embody our stories, and gently leads us into the empowering territory of a naturally gracious way of being."
—**Rayona Sharpnack**, Founder and CEO of the Institute for Women's Leadership and member of the Women's Leadership Board of the John F. Kennedy School of Government at Harvard University

"Victoria Castle writes from the heart of her own experience, giving a taste of what abundance feels like, *and* a set of Somatic practices that lead readers to transform this state into a permanent trait. This book is a gem!"
—**Dana Carman**, founding partner of Pacific Integral, Organizational Consultant, Educator, and Social Activist

The TRANCE *of* SCARCITY

HEY! STOP HOLDING YOUR BREATH
AND START LIVING YOUR LIFE

Jenell~
Here's to an
abundant life of
love, joy + peace!
Best to you,
Victoria

VICTORIA CASTLE

THE TRANCE OF SCARCITY

Published by
SAGACIOUS PRESS
P.O.Box 1001
Clinton, WA 98236

FIRST EDITION

Cover and Interior Design by Robert Lanphear
Illustrations by Obadinah Heavner

Library of Congress Cataloging-in-Publication Data.
Castle, Victoria
The trance of scarcity : hey! stop holding your breath
and start living your life / Victoria Castle.
Library of Congress Control Number: 2005931442
ISBN 0-9771331-0-9
1. Self-help. 2. Leadership. 3. Mind and Body.
4. Spirituality. 5. Wealth Building.

I. Title: The Trance of Scarcity. II. Title
10 9 8 7 6 5 4 3 2 1

CONTENTS

*May ours be the last generation
ensnared by the Trance of Scarcity*

Acknowledgments

I always like reading this page in books—it's both personal and public. Even offering my public thanks, however, feels insufficient to convey my gratitude to the brilliant, generous, talented, and loving individuals who have bestowed great gifts on me, whether they knew it or not. Some I have the privilege of knowing personally; others have stirred and informed me through their work. All have had a hand in this book, and I am profoundly grateful to them all.

Albert Einstein, R. Buckminster Fuller, Arnold Patent, Eric Butterworth, Brother David Steindl-Rast, Margaret Wheatley, Peter Senge, Peter Block, Warren Bennis, Jean Houston, Pema Chödron, Edwene Gaines, Riane Eisler, Vicki Robin, Lynne Twist, Humberto Maturana, Thomas Berry, Fernando Flores, Rupert Sheldrake, George Leonard, Desmond Tutu, Mohammed Junus, Anne Lamott, Mary Oliver, David Whyte, Tom Robbins.

Richard Strozzi-Heckler, Staci Haines, Denise Benson, Paula Love, Julia Smith, Rick Head, Phil Hallstein, Brooke Beazley, Mary Michael Wagner, Anna Scott, Linda Spencer, David MacArthur, Jerilyn Brusseau, Donna Zajonc, Carol Winkler, David Womeldorff, David Hager, Bob Linz, Joanna Gabriel, Sabine Grandke-Taft, Gretchen Lawlor, Richard Rianoshek, Rayona Sharpnack, Lois Fein, Joel and Michelle Levey, Jamal Rahman, Catherin Maxwell, Ann Stadler, Vivienne Hull, Fritz Hull, Tracy Robinson, Marilyn Overcast, Yvonne Zick.

All my students and clients over the years, whose appetite and courage have inspired me, stretched me, and emboldened me to share this work.

My editor, Ceci Miller (www.CeciBooks.com), whose vision,

impeccability, savvy, and heart insured this material became the book it was called to be. Oh, that everyone could have such a guide!

My partner, Tim Morley: wizard, healer, lover, who from the minute we met encouraged me to "get out there and tell 'em the truth." Every day he shows me the depth of unconditional love and the importance of a sense of humor. My parents, Jack and Mac, who raised me to question the unquestionable as long as I had a darn good reason. And to Ginger and Tucker, the four-legged masters who have gently shown me the way to my humanity.

The TRANCE
of SCARCITY

HEY! STOP HOLDING YOUR BREATH
AND START LIVING YOUR LIFE

Introduction

What eclipses people's greatness? What stops us short from being as creative, caring, and resilient as we are? What is it that squeezes the life out of us so stealthily that we volunteer to shrink to a shadow of our true selves? And most importantly, how do we stop it?

Before we can decide on a treatment, we must first find the *source* of the malaise. Once Albert Einstein was presented with the following scenario: If you had one hour to solve a difficult problem, how would you use the time? He answered, "I'd spend the first 55 minutes defining the problem." In my own life, thoroughly defining the problem presented by the Trance of Scarcity took quite a bit longer than 55 minutes! But while my research may not have been comfortable or brief, it revealed to me an element of our existence, a *way of being*, that is most often invisible to us. Yet it fairly floats in the air we breathe. We catch it like a virus as we move within our cultural and familial surroundings, but then, strangely, we keep it alive for years without realizing how much better we would feel without it.

In working with thousands of people, I have repeatedly encountered the tragic theme of *I am not enough*—not good enough, smart enough, rich enough, young enough, old enough, worthy enough. Almost as prevalent is the theme of *There is not enough*—not enough time, money, opportunity, love, cooperation, power, you name it. This prevailing premise of *not-enough-ness* successfully cripples the lives of people who would otherwise be buoyant and passionate. Since its subjects are so readily yet unwittingly loyal to it, I came to call this blight the Trance of Scarcity.

A trance is a semi-conscious state, a daze, a predisposition: under its spell we accept what we're told without question. The Trance of Scarcity shows up in a hundred personalized versions, but the results are always the same. Instead of experiencing the brilliance and creativity we are aching to offer, the world gets the by-products of actions that oppress, isolate, exclude, and defeat.

The Trance of Scarcity has us in its snare and produces unfathomable waste. The Trance may show up privately, as self-doubt and over-consumerism, or publicly, as elitism and disregard for future generations. Many of us spend our time lamenting the way things are, justifying all the reasons why they can't be different, and preparing for the worst. Whether we act as the oppressed or the oppressor, we are caught in a web of our own making. As a reigning planetary myth, the Trance effectively keeps us from living at peace with ourselves and each other.

There is life on the other side of the Trance—a life characterized by vitality, fulfillment, and efficacy. It's not a pipe dream, and it's not as far away as we've been led to believe. It does, however, require tampering a bit with our beliefs and confronting whatever has lived within us as the stone cold truth (usually the most disruptive things we can imagine!). But then, claiming one's freedom always causes a certain degree of disruption. Breaking free is the polar opposite of comfort and stasis, very different from sedating ourselves so we can tolerate captivity.

To successfully upgrade from scarcity and struggle to Abundance and ease, we must interrupt and dislodge old patterns that have been living quite comfortably within us, acting like they own the place. These old patterns are like a cat that likes to sleep on your head but isn't the least bit interested in the fact that you are allergic. It's time to move the cat. A little discomfort can end a lifetime of suffering.

The more each of us chooses to live and breathe and move within a reality of sufficiency and inclusion, the quicker we will break the Trance that now holds our world in its sway. We end this disastrous tale when we stop telling it to ourselves and each other, when we literally begin to embody a better reality. The Trance loses its power when we address the *source* of the suffering rather than applying yet another bandage to the symptoms. We can eliminate this suffering, one person at a time, starting now.

This book will help you break free from the Trance of Scarcity in three ways.

1. By defying the cultural "common sense" that scarcity is an unchangeable truth, and revealing it for what it is—a mere story. Rather than offer strategies for better living in a world of scarcity, we will address the *source* of the "reality of scarcity" and expose it as a hoax, thus eliminating its power over us.

2. By leveraging the two elements that create our personal realities— our Stories and how we embody them—and then using those elements to create the reality we want. Insights and platitudes have too little impact on our lived experience; it is the practical essentials of *embodiment* that lead us to a new and sustained *way of being* where Abundance is readily at hand. Embodiment is a key player in living beyond the Trance and will be illustrated in detail.

3. By using the powerful, well-tested practices of the Cycle of Abundance that result in greater ease, freedom, and satisfaction. Through these practices—as relevant to organizations as they are to individuals—you will learn to literally embody the state of Abundance, of living in the world with greater effectiveness and ease.

Part I of this book looks at the roots of the Trance of Scarcity and the social constructs that hold it in place. We will then explore what generates your own reality and how you can change it at the most essential level, rather than waste another minute trying to get your circumstances to behave. Our focus here is on cultivating the *way of being* that aligns us with Abundance: the state of ease and flow.

You can live your life so that you're never captured or crippled by circumstances again. Embodying Abundance isn't like a fad diet, it's a *way of being* firmly grounded in what actually works. It means that no matter what life presents, you can embody confidence, resilience, and success—not because you're more deserving but because you've found the leverage point for real freedom. It's a whole new ball game, and one that people miss out on when they maintain blind allegiance to the Trance of Scarcity, which insists that *there is never enough, regardless.*

After a lifetime of struggle and strain, we become suspicious of pleasure, ease, and flow. According to the Trance, the tighter we're wound the better. But ironically, this contraction of mind and body is the perfect breeding ground for scarcity.

In Part II, we'll investigate how the most important ally to embodying Abundance is (*oh no!*) pleasure. We're talking about real pleasure—not the shallow kind that comes from overindulgence but rather the capacity to be so fully present to our lives that we partake of their richness in a way that feeds the soul. The original root of the word *pleasure* means *supple*, like a river freely flowing or a fabric with give and resilience. Abundance thrives on flow, not constriction. Specific practices are offered in this book that will show you how to embody this flow.

What we embody becomes our *way of being*; it influences every part of us. Our *way of being* in the world is the result of what we practice, whether or not it is intentional. Our habits and automatic reactions live in our muscles and in our nervous system. That's why the conceptual approach of "mind over matter" does little more than irritate—it cannot override what is already embodied. Some behaviors and habits are the result of years of embodying our unexamined Stories (such as the Trance of Scarcity), and they hold us in patterns that run counter to our biggest commitments; patterns such as believing we're not good enough, waiting for circumstances to change so we can be successful, and accumulating enough stuff that we feel safe.

The good news is we already have all the technology we need to make the fundamental shift away from the Trance of Scarcity and into Embodied Abundance. By engaging in the practices offered in this book, we can release our habitual embodiment of the Trance. We can change our experience from a life dominated by struggle and constriction to a life of greater ease and possibility. And this shift can occur *independent* of our circumstances.

Embodied Abundance goes far beyond the narcissistic orientation of "As long as I have what I need, that's all that matters." Real Abundance means living in a state of fullness and flow, welcoming our interconnectedness with everyone else. This is the great power of breaking free from the Trance of Scarcity. Little by little, we are released from the Me orientation that has kept us separate and lonely, and we enter the We orientation that makes room for our hearts and minds to stay open and connected.

In addition to working with my clients and students, I have personally, in excruciating detail, tested all of the principles presented here. About 20 years ago I went through a year I now affectionately refer to as Victoria's Adventures in Hell. At the time, I just called it Hell. In a matter of months I went though a crushing divorce, my father died, I had surgery for a major health risk, I moved to a new city where I knew no one, I looked for work for six months, and day by day I watched the little money I had disappear. I was well down the path of permanent suffering and struggle when, much to my surprise, I found a different route and took it. Since then my focus has been on embodying what I learned during that time and making it accessible to others, with the hope that their own Adventures in Hell might be as short-lived as possible. This book includes plenty of stories from my own experience, for your education . . . and amusement.

What I learned was this simple but crucial formula: What we believe and what we embody becomes our reality. If we address both causes, our lives change. While the power of belief has been recognized for years, embodiment has been overlooked, even though it is essential to lasting change. Anything short of embodiment is just chatter.

As I caught sight of the Trance of Scarcity quietly pulling my strings, I realized that it was pervasive in far more lives than mine. The Trance has proven itself to be pandemic. In individuals, communities, organizations, systems, and governments, it has become institutionalized and is accepted without question. Learning to free ourselves is both a personal and planetary issue, if we are to create a future in which we all can thrive.

When one person gains access to her greatness, we all benefit. The essentials of Embodied Abundance aren't sneaky or slippery, they're hidden only as long as we look at life through the lens of the Trance of Scarcity. We keep seeing the hopeless view conjured by *not enough*, and eventually, being thoroughly convinced that the whole thing is pointless, we stop looking.

At this period in history, the majority of people throughout the world feel disempowered and exhausted. Doesn't make for a very bright future, does it? We know all too well what life looks like inside the Trance of Scarcity—the evidence is everywhere we turn. The time is right to see what life is like when we live in freedom from the Trance. Fulfilled people—those who have ready access to their greatness and aliveness—are resourceful, generous, resilient, peace-making folk. A world full of such people has a very different future than the one we face now. Each one of us holds a piece of the larger solution. Each of us plays our part by making the contribution that is ours alone to make, the one that we're itching to bring forth. That's where the real fun is.

If you have had enough struggle, if you are ready for greater autonomy and aliveness, read on. You'll be helping to change the world, whether you intend to or not. Once you embody Abundance as your *way of being*, you can't help but be more inspired and more inspiring. You'll build bridges to replace dead ends, and you'll easily arrive at solutions to issues that used to overwhelm you. You'll have broken free from the Trance of Scarcity, and your bountiful life will show it clearly to anyone who wants the same.

PART I

STATE

If struggling were the way to get there,
we'd all be there by now.

Chapter

1

Belonging:
Are You In or Out?

Chances are you're a master at reading situations to see where and how you can belong. It's hardwired into us as human beings. Of all the mammals on earth, we spend the greatest length of time dependent on others. Our survival depends on our being included, cared for, and accepted so that we belong in our tribe. We get very good at noticing how we must behave in order to be included. Even when we've moved past the risk of biological need, we remain watchful: "Am I in or out?" Teenagers experience this questioning particularly intensely; that's probably why very few of us would want to repeat our teen years.

Most of us have been bombarded with religious and cultural messages about what it takes to belong, who decides whether or not we belong, and what might threaten our belonging. In all our choices, the issue of belonging stands in the background, whether or not we're aware of it. For most of us, wanting to belong runs the whole show. The trouble is, most of us are convinced that we didn't make the cut, that we don't belong, so we spend all our time either auditioning for others' approval, hoping we'll be included, or pretending not to care whether we're in or out. At the bottom of all this suffering lies the Trance of Scarcity.

A reporter once asked Albert Einstein, "Dr. Einstein, if you could ask the universe a single question and receive a direct reply, what would you ask?"

His response was immediate, as though he had been pondering it for quite some time. "Is the universe friendly?"

What is your answer to this essential question? It's worth noting. How we answer this question forms the basis of our response to all that we encounter in our lives. Whether or not we allow ourselves in or out of any given situation depends on it.

If we answer that the universe is *not* friendly, we hold ourselves at the mercy of imagined hostile external forces; we feel we're strictly on our own. This belief impoverishes every area of our lives. And we're not the only ones feeling this way. For centuries, humanity has been marinating in such messages, sometimes provided by religion, sometimes by society at large—insisting that we're unworthy outsiders, that we must earn our way to belonging.

Bound by this message, we feel alone, ashamed, permanently insufficient. We move through the world like dejected spectators: strained, isolated, telling ourselves story after story of our unworthiness and life's unfairness. Feeding on a continual diet of despair and rejection, courtesy of the Trance of Scarcity, we desperately seek ways to go numb. Our life force is gradually diminished to a whisper.

If we answer that the universe *is* friendly, however, we show up at the party ready to greet old friends and meet new ones. We add our signature dish to the potluck and prepare to feast. We understand that partaking of the flow takes nothing away from anyone else. We freely partake of and freely contribute to the constant stream of resources and possibilities. Our belonging is undisputed. No longer auditioning, we're confirmed in our right to exist. We live with a sense of freedom and possibility. We create a life of meaning and fulfillment, absorbed in making the unique contribution to the human community that is ours to make.

Step Into the Circle

Imagine you're walking in open country. You come upon a vast Circle in an expansive, fertile field. Streams and springs are flowing into this sunny area, providing the optimal environment for life to flourish. This is not a Circle made by human hands; rather, it's a zone where the energy of the universe flows without restriction. The Circle is not made or run by people, though everyone and everything is included in it. You have your own permanent place here. Just looking around, smelling the fresh scent of the natural world, feeling the sun on your skin, it feels good to be here.

The Circle is home to a flow of satisfying relationships, meaningful work, inspired learning, endless resources and opportunities, laughter and creativity, and a prevailing sense of ease. Remember a time when you felt carefree, safe, energized, and happy—maybe building a fort with some friends as a kid, or dancing with your sweetheart. That's the feeling: a pervasive sense of glad assurance. In the Circle, life is not a series of obstacles to overcome; it's a steady flow of possibilities.

There is no fence around this Circle, no admission gate, no entrance fee. Regardless of your age, your weight, the color of your skin, your gender, your education, your nationality, your financial status, or other people's opinions of you—you already belong here. No person or condition has the power to keep you out. You alone can take yourself out of the Circle, but your place will always be reserved for you. Your place in the Circle never expires. If you leave, it's simply vacant until you return.

So come on in. Or you may find that you don't have to move at all, the Circle expands to include you. The Circle can be as spacious or cozy as you like. Set down all the baggage you've been

carrying. Isn't it nice to be rid of that burden? Your shoulders relax, you take a deep breath, and your back uncoils. The tension begins to subside in your stomach and neck. It's like getting into a hot tub after a long rainy trudge on a winter's day. When you're ready, take time to wander all over the Circle until you find the spot you like best. You can stand, sit, lie down, walk, turn cartwheels, whatever you choose to do. The nature of the Circle is flow, and you are part of that flow wherever you are and whatever you do within the Circle. There is nothing here that you must force or control.

Here are some reports of how it feels to reside inside the Circle.

"I'm smarter, funnier, and I'm sure better-looking."

"Colors are brighter and I feel alive, like when I hiked Mount Rainier."

"Now I know why our puppy is happy all the time!"

"I realize I've been on a deprivation diet my whole life. And it turns out there's a banquet being served 24 hours a day. I'm having seconds!"

"An oasis in the desert . . . Now I get what that means."

"Problems really do become opportunities here."

"I hesitate to give up my pessimism, but it seems like nothing's out of reach here."

"I had no idea how clenched I was. The more I open up, the better it gets!"

"The only restriction on what's possible is how much good I can stand!"

For a moment now, purposefully yank yourself out of the Circle. Stand at a distance, looking at the Circle but no longer inside it. Notice how you feel when you take yourself out and separate yourself. You may feel lonely, separate, left out, invisible, or disconnected. Being outside the Circle may also feel familiar, while being inside may feel like a wild, unlikely fantasy. If you're used to struggle, ease can feel foreign and you may distrust it at first.

. . . .

Connectedness is an organizing principle of the universe.

David Boehm

. . . .

Now come back into the Circle and once again make yourself at home in the way that feels best for you. For some, being in the Circle may feel like "too much," and you may actually feel more comfortable outside. Honor your own pace. You might begin by moving closer to the Circle and just checking it out. Then you might move toward the edge, and later step just barely inside. This practice entails finding where you have greatest access to your aliveness, to your endless resources. There's no wrong way to consent to becoming part of the Circle. Simply discover what works for you. Just know that *you already belong* and that your space is always reserved for you, no matter what.

The nature of the Circle is flow, so whenever you step into the Circle, you step into the flow. When you're out of the Circle, separate, you're resisting the flow. Remember: There's no way to earn your way into the Circle because you already belong.

Stepping into the Circle isn't determined by your worthiness. It depends on your consent.

*Feeding on a continual diet of despair and rejection courtesy
of the Trance of Scarcity, we desperately seek ways to go
numb. Our life force is gradually diminished to a whisper.*

Can you hear a loud chorus right now saying, "Yeah, right, nice fantasy! Now let's get back to the real world, shall we?" Could this be your *Do Not Disturb the Comfort Zone* alarm going off? Hang on for a moment, now, and just check this out. What would it be like if you lived—all the time—as if you already belonged?

Notice that last bit. We're not just consumers in this Circle. We are generators, far more ingenious, inspired, and outrageously collaborative than we could have imagined. The Circle is enriched because we're in it.

· · · · · · ·

*From the moment we cease trying to swim upstream and begin to
flow with the current, something changes in us.*

Arthur Sokoloff

· · · · · · ·

Let's be clear: the Circle is not a place. It doesn't have a time zone or a compass point. The Circle is a *way of being*—and we're either *being* in the Circle or *being* out of the Circle. Most of us have thoroughly embodied a *way of being* outside of the Circle. I did. It was from this vantage point that I discovered the Circle. I kept seeing this other reality in the distance, and I kept wondering what you had to do to be eligible to get in. It couldn't possibly be open to *everyone*. It couldn't possibly be open to *me*. I was raised on a common assortment of mantras: *There's Not Enough; Settle for Less; Wait Your Turn; Fight Like Hell for What You Want.*

No matter which of these phrases I chose, there was an implied atmosphere of competition and combat, of domination and intimidation. To dominate or intimidate, it's necessary to create a sense of scarcity. (We'll explore this further in the next chapter.) Of course, my parents' objective was not to dominate or intimidate me (though there were surely times they would have welcomed help subduing their unruly offspring). They were doing their best to prepare me for what they believed were the harsh realities of life, to toughen me up so I could survive in a world of scarcity and struggle.

Not enough thinking keeps us in survival mode, our reptilian brain on constant alert, scanning for threats, preparing to attack or defend. *Not enough* thinking preempts our higher brain functions, the ones that inspire us to innovate and cooperate.

Now here's where the Trance gets tricky. If we believe that being separate is the way to be safe, then we'll create distance between ourselves and others; we'll refuse to count on anyone; we'll isolate ourselves. There are two corners into which we can wedge ourselves so that we remain separate. Both of them are inauthentic due to the fact that we're hard-wired to relate to and connect with life. In one corner we can decide to be a victim. Our theme song becomes "You done me wrong just like I always knew you would." In the other corner we can decide to be a hero or a martyr. Whichever corner we stand in—victim or hero/martyr—we're operating out of separation.

Preparing for Struggle Perpetuates Struggle

Let's go back to the Circle now. Remember: No one can keep you out but you. There's no fence, no gate, no ticket taker. No one but you can take yourself out of the Circle, and most of us do so hundreds of times a day. To get out quickly, here are several accelerated routes: *I'm not enough. There is not enough. This can never work. It's impossible. It's too late. Nobody cares. It's too hard. I don't deserve it. I don't belong.* Accelerated routes out of the Circle can also take these forms: *shallow or no breathing, slumped shoulders, furrowed brow, tense neck, clenched jaw,* and *collapsed chest.* Whether you leave the Circle by way of internal messages or by way of physical constriction, the result is the same. Scarcity and struggle take hold.

. . . .

If my aim is to prove I am "enough," the project goes on to infinity because the battle was already lost on the day I conceded the issue was debatable.

Nathaniel Brandon

. . . .

Whenever we constrict the flow of life force by clenching our bodies or by telling ourselves limiting Stories, we are practicing separation rather than belonging—and that takes us out of the Circle. When we feel stingy, judgmental, defeated, self-righteous, or victimized, we've stepped out of the Circle. When we open up, relax, and join in, we have stepped into the Circle, and we experience the warmth and delight of being in the flow.

So, you may be saying, if there are accelerated routes out of the Circle, there must also be a quick way or two of getting back in. And indeed, this is the case. It's a very short list: Give your consent.

This is all that's required to come back into the Circle—only your consent. The Latin root word for *consent, consentire,* means *to join with feeling.* Perfect, isn't it? We experience being either in or out of the Circle according to how we *feel,* how we *are,* according to what we say is so.

Choosing to belong in the Circle is an act of sovereignty. We belong because we choose to belong. We don't force or demand it because that would mean we were still playing the eligibility game. Consent is simply accepting our place in the flow of life. It's a choice made from moment to moment. So here's the practice: Whenever you notice you've stepped out of the Circle, consent to come back in.

·······

Spirituality is belonging to something greater than yourself.

Brother David Steindl-Rast

·······

Taking your place in the Circle means belonging to the flow of all life, joining with it, drawing on its juice and vitality, and making your own contribution to it. Stepping into the Circle means hooking up your individual life force with a life force much bigger than yours—the life force that moves and fuels all things.

The Circle is only one image, of course. If it's useful to you, great. If it's distracting, find an image that works better for you. Why did I choose a circle and not a river, you ask? Because, like the Cycle of Abundance, the flow constantly replenishes itself.

The Cycle of Abundance works like the breath; there's inhalation and exhalation. So where is the starting point, the ending point? Exactly! There isn't one. Being part of the Circle gives you access to everything that is flowing through life, and whatever you bring with you becomes part of the flow. You're not just an insignificant gnat flying around in the vast circle of infinity—what you bring into the Circle matters. It's part of the character of the whole. It's a good reason not to vacate your post.

In his powerful book *No Future without Forgiveness*, Desmond Tutu shares the concept of *ubuntu*. In African culture, *ubuntu* is our interconnectedness with all of life, as well as the responsibility inherent in our connection. It might be translated this way: "I am human because I belong." I don't belong because I am human, but the other way around. Belonging is understood as the very essence of humanity.

PRACTICE
Choosing to Belong
. . . .

Since we're exploring *embodied* Abundance (not conceptual abundance), here's our first Somatic practice. Remember: What you practice, you become!

1. Read the description of the Circle at the beginning of this chapter, or close your eyes and visualize your own Circle image. Make it a visceral experience. What does it feel like in your belly, in your feet, in your throat, to belong to the Circle? Really take time to wander around in this inner experience until you find the *way of being* in the Circle that feels best to you. And—this is important—there is no one right way to be there.

   Spend a few moments there, just getting used to being in the flow without needing to make anything happen. It may feel very foreign; most of us have been nosing that grindstone for decades. You might even feel a little bit idle; that's okay. Relax and enjoy. You're in the midst of the flow; everything comes right to where you are. It flows through you, and then out from you. Effortlessly.

2. Now bring your attention to your concerns about the future. Maybe you sense a lack of money or a lack of self-worth. Maybe you remember your problems at work or at home, or how much you have to do, or how unfair life is. Notice how all this feels in your body. In particular, notice your breath, your level of tension, your degree of aliveness.

Chances are good that when you began considering the future, you just propelled yourself out of the Circle. So take a moment to feel what it's like to be distant, to be out of the flow, to be separate from the rest of life. What's your degree of aliveness? It may feel quite familiar. If you've spent 20, 30, 40, or 50 years outside the Circle, then being outside feels like business as usual.

3. When you've had enough of that, take a deep breath and consciously consent to rejoining the Circle. You might say this out loud or simply think the words to yourself. Recognize that you are the only one who has the authority to take yourself out of the Circle. You are automatically a part of the Circle, if you consent to be. You have dominion here. You make the choice. Now, one more time, quietly notice how it feels here. What is your breathing like? How tense or relaxed are you? What feels possible from this vantage point? What is your degree of aliveness at this moment? If being in the Circle feels a little foreign to you, just take it slowly. Gradually keep coming back to the orientation of joining the flow of life energy and endless possibility.

4. Repeat this practice several times, making it more vivid and visceral each time. Go at your own pace, until being in the Circle feels like home.

What if we lived as if we already belonged?

Chapter 2

The Trance of Scarcity: Our Sad Story

I'm 55, and I want to feel alive." Outwardly, Barbara was successful in every sense of the word, but secretly her life felt desolate. "I've done everything I know to do, but it feels like my energy just keeps getting siphoned off somehow. What do I have to do to finally be *good enough*?" With these words, she revealed that she was living outside the Circle on a full-time basis.

Barbara's question seared me right to the bone. It's a question that goes to the heart of the matter for a great many of us. What must we do to feel, at long last, that we're *enough* as we are? Is it ever possible to feel a sense of true belonging, to resign from our careers of self-improvement? Or is our only option to join the Stoics of ancient Greece who believed that humans should be free of passion and accept all occurrences with indifference? Seems to me the last thing the world needs is *more* indifference!

Most of us have developed a Herculean tolerance for suffering. And we put up with far more of it than what is biologically wired into our nervous system, as part of our internal survival gear. Our survival instinct increases our awareness of stimulus, especially pain, alerting us to adjust to conditions as they occur. *Pssst, feel that burning in your hand. Let go of the electric fence!* But if we believe that no adjustment would help (if letting go of the fence is not an option), we keep turning down the volume on our sense of aliveness. If we believe our pain or difficulty to be inescapable, we numb out in desperation. Like Barbara, we may keep trying harder and harder to follow the wrong prescription, attempting to cure ourselves of being ourselves. And it's all we know to do; we've spent years designing our entire life according to what we believe is real. Our belief in scarcity shows up in our bodies as a lack of aliveness, and in our lives as the experience of lack and limitation.

This is where the mischief begins. We're not always great at assessing what's real and what isn't. See if any of these statements sound familiar: *I'm not enough. There's never enough to go around. It's so hard. Nothing comes easy. That'll never work.* Most of us have been repeating such statements to ourselves for decades, and as far as we know they accurately describe reality. Really, though, they're just ideas.

Ideas like these, in time, become a big part of who we think we are. At this point, the thought "I'm not enough" or "There's never enough" is no longer a thought; it lives as the Truth (and we're convinced that everybody else accepts that Truth, too). We'll actually defend these statements, no matter how lousy it feels to believe them, because we've built our whole reality on them. They're our foundation, our security. Without them, how will we know what's what?

· · · · · · ·

Argue for your limitations and they are yours.

Richard Bach

· · · · · · ·

Human beings are natural storytellers, and we are most captivated by the Stories we tell ourselves. An event occurs, and right away we go about the business of interpretation. We assign some meaning to the event. Once we've assigned a meaning (and we've deemed ourselves to be correct), we forget that there might be other possible interpretations of the same event. We then pass on our conclusions to our neighbors and children and students. And here's the trouble: If *they* don't recognize our truth as a mere interpretation or a Story—our personal perception of things—then they, too, treat the Story as though it's the Truth. They move right in and set up house inside it. Now the Story may persist for centuries, generation after generation, as though chiseled into the side of a mountain.

Trances Are Sneaky

A trance is a semi-conscious state that operates in our lives without question or discernment. It becomes our way of living, directing our actions according to whatever programming is featured in the trance. Living entranced is the opposite of living in sovereignty, of being self-governing. Stage hypnotists are famous for inducing trance states in which people act in ways they would be unlikely to act when fully awake. A trance can be a source of entertainment, or a source of suffering.

> ### The Trance of Scarcity
> *The unexamined predisposition that lack, struggle, and separation are our defining reality.*

Every day we are offered increasingly sophisticated strategies for surviving in a world of scarcity. No one questions whether scarcity exists. All such survival strategies share the same starting point: They accept scarcity (lack of self-worth and lack of resources) as a fact of life, as the only proper orientation in response to the evidence. But what if the truth were actually the other way around? **What if our default way of thinking—maintaining the idea that scarcity is real—is the *source* of the conditions producing the "evidence"?** Which one's the chicken and which one's the egg?

· · · · · · ·

People only see what they are prepared to see.

Ralph Waldo Emerson

· · · · · · ·

Many years ago Albert Einstein pointed to the limitations of the mind, saying that we can't seek to solve problems within the same mindset that created them. To defeat this way of seeking, we must become a little bit radical and impertinent. I say *radical* because when we try to crack an illusion, our denial often intensifies in order to protect our familiar reality. It takes courage not to sit with folded hands at our desks and accept that red is actually green—especially when everyone else in class is pointing to the fire engine and saying, "Of *course* it's green. What are you, *crazy?!*" In an atmosphere like that, it takes courage even to allow ourselves to get curious about the persistent predisposition. So at this point I'm not asking you to accept that a Trance of Scarcity exists. For now I'm just inviting you to join me in considering the possibility. *What if there is a Trance of Scarcity? What if that Trance is the source of much of the world's suffering?* What are the ramifications? What are the possibilities

Bernard Lietaer, author of *The Future of Money* and co-designer of the single European currency system, has studied and operated in the international currency system for decades. He says, "If a society is afraid of scarcity, it will actually create an environment in which it manifests well-grounded reasons to live in fear of scarcity. It is a self-fulfilling prophecy!" Might you be familiar with such a society?

When we sustain fear or anxiety for long periods of time, we lose access to our higher brain functions.

When I spoke on this subject at the Seattle Chapter of the Institute of Noetic Sciences, we discussed the origins of the Trance. It became obvious that even these innovative thinkers had not really considered scarcity as a kind of trance—something we think without really thinking. I realized then that this Trance is sneaky, that it has been flying under the radar. For this reason, very few of us have even considered its existence and impact on humanity, much less how to break free from it.

·······

The most suppressive forces are the ones
no one knows are at work.

Ken Anbender

·······

Our Stories Create Our World

Is the Trance a newcomer in our lifetime? Hardly. It's the result of multiple messages and interpretations over time. Here are some of the prime influences on our current experience in Western civilization. Notice how they have contributed to the Trance of Scarcity remaining unquestioned.

- **When humans sustain fear or anxiety for long periods of time, we lose access to our higher brain functions**—our capacity to create and collaborate, to be curious or compassionate. Unable to respond spontaneously in the present moment, we continue responding based on whatever past conditioning remains lodged in our system. And the result is not pretty. As well as eroding our physical well-being, sustained fear creates a petri dish of conditions in which prejudice, suspicion, hoarding, isolation, and self-justification flourish.

- **Human beings are storytellers.** The instant decree of "This is the way it is, and this is how we're going to deal with it" both ensures our survival and fosters our limitations. Just for a moment, think about dogs. You have an instant response. You like dogs or you don't like them, or maybe they scare you. You think they're a nuisance or they're cute, and so on. Some earlier decree made by you or your family is already well in place; all you had to do was turn your attention to that area of your conditioning, and you knew exactly how to feel about dogs. *Ta da!* Instant story.

- The Greek civilization (600 BCE–300 BCE) profoundly shaped Western culture. The virtues revered by the Greeks included **being a good citizen and living a refined life**. This was the approved way to live. Those who did not adopt this way of being were assigned less power and status.

- By the 17th century, Descartes' Rationalism and Newtonian physics had separated spirit from matter and explained life as mechanistic. Cartesian thinking taught that the **mind mattered most**, and urged us to ignore emotions and sensations. Things were black or white, one way or another—the world became binary. As we studied the great thoughts of others, we moved away from attending to and trusting our firsthand experience, having accepted that everything worth knowing, everything true and real, was found outside us.

- The Puritans and Calvinists who settled the early American colonies endeavored relentlessly to be good enough due to their belief that **we were inherently flawed and insufficient.**

- Adam Smith defined modern economics as a way of allocating scarce resources through the mechanism of individual, personal greed. From his observations, he deduced that **greed and scarcity were the operating principles of all "civilized" societies.**

- In a capitalist culture, competition is encouraged, but with the caveat that **not everyone can win.** Advertising and the media send us a consistent message: We are lacking and we must constantly do more and acquire more in order to erase this lack. Darwin's theory of evolution confirmed our biological imperative to strive constantly, to eat or be eaten.

At this juncture in history our daily lives continue to be dictated, in large part, by these ideas—they live unquestioned. Yes, we are biological beings, always alert to getting our needs met. Yes, we are storytellers, and what we tell ourselves creates our world. And yes, we share the world with other human beings, many of whom have internalized a similar story about *not being enough*. So it's likely we will continue to encounter struggles for power and control.

As satisfying as it might be to track down the culprit who started the nasty story of scarcity, it's not as though the Trance was created maliciously. And even if we did identify the source, it doesn't change anything. What's most important is finding the leverage point that will free us to make our unique contributions and to live in the world with ease. Not all cultures have a prevailing story about scarcity. That fact lends hope to our cause. We *can* disperse the fog that blurs our vision and cramps our style.

· · · · · · ·

The world is made up of stories, not atoms.

Muriel Rukeyser

· · · · · · ·

How a Story Works

How did you come by your beliefs about Abundance and scarcity, about money, about your self-worth, about what you deserve, about what's possible? Can you trace them to their origin? Some beliefs were transferred to us like precious family heirlooms to be guarded and tended for posterity. For most of us, though, these beliefs have simply been *always there*. Like air. We never questioned their validity and permanency in our lives. But we're questioning them now, to see whether they serve our highest intentions, or hold us back. How do I know that telling stories comes naturally? Read on.

I was a sophomore in high school, riding a roller coaster of low self-esteem and high drama. One Friday night after a football game, there was a dance sponsored by the county's three high schools. My girlfriends and I glossed our lips and readied ourselves to meet the guys of our dreams.

We stepped into the gym and were greeted by a blast of hormones moving to the beat. Thank goodness, people were actually dancing—something I did well. In no time at all, one of the guys from the cool high school asked me to dance. We moved easily together and kept dancing, song after song, the slow dances not lasting long enough. A cute upperclassman, and a good dancer! He met all my requirements. As the last song ended, he asked for my phone number and said, "I'll call you."

Dating had begun. I was officially "in," a member of the inner circle, of girls who went on dates. He liked me. He was going to call me. We'd go out, date for months, go steady, be devoted to each other. I went to sleep that night thrilled about my future. "Happily ever after" was at last in sight.

Saturday morning I made my nest by the phone. Whenever the phone rang, I pounced like a tigress and, discovering it wasn't him, quickly dismissed the caller. The entire day passed. Pouncing, dismissing. No call from the cute upperclassman. But Sunday was a new day and a sure bet, and I resumed my vigil. Evening arrived. No call.

Monday's telephone duty was interrupted by school, but I was back at my post by early evening. Monday and Tuesday passed. No call. I checked and double-checked to make sure the line wasn't dead.

So this is what Hell feels like. Now I knew the truth. He was laughing with his friends right now about this dumb girl he was certainly *never* going to call. What a fool I was!

Out of desperation, I worked up my nerve to seek my older brother's counsel. (He was a senior and knew just about everything.) At the threshold of my brother's bedroom door I stopped, my chin buttoned to my chest. He was sitting at his desk doing homework. I choked out, "Marshall, can I ask you a question?"

"What?" He leaned back and shrugged his upperclassman shrug.

"If a guy said he was going to call you, but then he didn't call . . . what does that mean?"

I braced myself for the impact—clenching the door jam, squeezing my eyes shut to protect myself from the devastating truth I was about to hear.

Without looking up, my brother said, "It means he didn't call."

What!? Oh my God, I thought, it's a male conspiracy, and even my heroic brother is part of it! He's not going to break the code, even for me. I'm doomed.

I found my way to my room and withered to the floor, where I was greeted by the void. All was lost. No hope, no future. I dove into the gloom and disintegrated. But then the strangest thought occurred to me: Maybe there was something to what my brother had just said. What did I actually know for a fact? One: I had given him my phone number. Two: He had said he would call. Three: He hadn't called. That was all I knew for sure. The rest was all my concoction. I headed back to my brother's room, in a haze of disbelief, to thank him.

PRACTICE
Examining Stories
• • • •

Now it's your turn to use your natural storytelling skills. Below are some Facts and accompanying Stories/Interpretations we might make from them. Add at least two of your own to each category. The possibilities are endless! Remember, there are no wrong answers, because these are just Stories they're never true.

Fact	Story/Interpretation
He didn't call	
	I'll never have a date
	He's nervous about calling me
	Men are liars
	He lost my number
	Life is cruel

There are calories in food
> I need to study nutrition
> All the good foods are fattening
> Food is the enemy
> Food is fuel that keeps me going

Our bank balance is $143.20
> We have plenty to share
> We never have enough
> We had a great month

I don't have a Master's degree
> I can't do the work I want to do
> I'm not smart enough
> Street smarts are more important
> My knowledge is practical

What came to your mind are the Stories you have residing in your ever-ready story bank. These keep replaying themselves as if they're the Truth, unless we remember that they're only Stories—a few of the many thousands we might have chosen to tell ourselves.

Have you noticed how we tend to get a little egocentric in our Stories? If something doesn't work out the way we want it to, we can quickly jump to the conclusion that things fell through because we're unworthy or have done something wrong. While this stance can seem self-effacing, we're also claiming that our personal unworthiness is the prime mover of life's circumstances—that the universe has organized itself around us! While our Puritan ancestors might be proud that we accept our lack of worth, they would surely cringe at our self-absorption.

. . . .

Born fictioneers, all of us, we quest for causes and explanations,
and if they don't come readily to hand, we make them up, because
a wrong answer is better than no answer.

Diane Ackerman

. . . .

Our storytelling skills are encoded in our DNA. When humans dwelled in caves and hunted for food, we had to think and act quickly to avoid danger, to stay alive. The cave dwellers who didn't excel at this skill weren't our ancestors— they were dinner! You're walking through the woods alone. You hear a twig snap behind you. In a split second you must decide what that means and what action to take. Human beings assign meaning; it's what we do. An event occurs, and in a nanosecond we interpret what that event means. Sometimes the story is useful, and sometimes it isn't.

The idea isn't to stop having opinions or interpretations (because we can't—they're wired in). Rather, **our goal is to stop mistaking our Stories for the Truth**. No matter how long they have been around or how many people believe them and never question them, Stories are still just Stories—they never graduate to become the Truth.

The good news is that we can change our Stories; they're not carved in stone. The world is made particle by particle, story by story. When I learned this distinction, my life was forever altered. I began to see my Stories everywhere. I had built shrines to many of them and worshiped them daily.

. . . .

Attention without intention can easily be manipulated.

James O'Dea

. . . .

At first, changing my long-held Stories felt like an act of treason. (I kept watching my back to be sure I didn't get caught.) But treason against whom? Against what? A trance? Why did I insist on remaining loyal to an idea that only kept me oppressed and fearful? At length I claimed my freedom without apology. A quiet act of revolution.

Remodeling Your Story

Imagine that when you moved into your first apartment, you inherited a rug that had been in your family for years. Since that day, you have brought it with you to every place you've lived for the last 20 years. The rug is so familiar that you really don't even see it anymore. It's not really part of the décor; it's just always been a part of your surroundings. One day you move into a house filled with light, and you see that the rug is really worn out and doesn't look so great anymore. It has been with you for a very long while, but the time has come to replace it with one that befits your fresh, new habitat.

You roll up the old rug and put it out for recycling. You search until you find a rug that is a real upgrade, that makes you feel good when you stand on it. You bring it home, and the whole place seems completely different. The rug's nice and thick, so much better than the old worn-out one. It's so plush that you actually trip on it a few times as you get used to walking on it. And every time you look at this new rug, you feel good.

When we upgrade, we are trading rug for rug, Story for Story. We're not trying to convince ourselves we can change the truth about ourselves by reciting endless affirmations. That hardly respects our intelligence and, furthermore, it doesn't work. As long as we hold that something is the truth, it is unchangeable. As soon as we recognize it for what it is however, a story, the story buffet line is open and we can help ourselves to a better one.

Regarding our Stories, the question is never "Is it true?" because it can't be true; it's just a Story. The question also isn't "Is it the right Story?" because that implies there's only one correct choice. The most helpful question is "Is this Story useful?" *Given what I care about, what I want to contribute, and what matters to me, is the story I'm telling myself a useful one?* Most of us constantly replay hundreds of inherited default Stories that trample our life energy and steal our peace of mind.

Below is a list of **Impoverishing Stories**. See if any of them have a familiar ring. How might you upgrade them?

I'll never be good enough

Life is unfair

If I have this, others won't

You have to work hard for everything you get

I'm only valuable when I am producing something

There's not enough time

It's too late

I should be different

I don't deserve a great life

I have to do everything myself

I must never disappoint anyone

I'm supposed to be perfect

No one in my family ever amounts to much

Why bother? I never make it anyway

Life is hard

Pleasure makes you lazy

Idle hands are the devil's workshop

I have to control everything to make things work out

I can't allow anything to go wrong on my watch
If I'm super-responsible, things will be okay
I can't ask for help
You have to hold on to anything you get
It's every man for himself
Some people are just better than others
It's all a matter of luck
I can never relax
We never have enough
Nothing ever works out for me
You can't have money and live a spiritual life
I'm the wrong gender, ethnicity, age, weight, etc.
What's the point?
Blessed are those who constantly struggle

Are you getting tired yet?

The work of Japanese scientist, Dr. Masaru Emoto, documents how molecules of water show the effects of our thoughts, words, and feelings. In his photographs, he shows water crystals that formed in bottles with different words written on them. Water exposed to positive messages formed beautiful hexagonal crystals, but water exposed to negative messages crystallized into chaotic, fragmented shapes. Since our bodies are 98 percent water, we too shape ourselves according to the messages in our surroundings.

In the next chapter, you'll learn how to upgrade any story that's not working for you. You'll discover the Stories that are defeating your true purpose, and trade them for Stories that bring your creativity, aliveness, and joy into full play.

What if scarcity is perpetuated by the Stories we tell ourselves?

Chapter 3

Upgrading Our Stories

You may find that you are ready to make a large leap or to take several small steps in upgrading your Stories. Either way will work just as well. Just step up to the story buffet line and pick out an upgraded Story. Put it on your plate, taste it, and see how you feel. If it's not quite the right taste, get a fresh plate and try another one. We live in such a binary world of either/or that we usually quit if we don't find the perfect fit right away (except, of course, for the recreational shoppers, whose infinite capacity to browse and experiment amazes and exhausts the rest of us). The point here is to keep going until you've found a Story that works for you. If next week you discover an even better upgrade, then great! Make a new trade. Your compass question remains: "**Given what I care about, is this story useful?**" Here's an example of one of my old Stories. I'll show you how I unpacked it and traded it in for a replacement.

What is one of my prevailing Stories?
• I don't deserve a great life

What are my actions and behaviors that keep that Story alive?
• I feel guilty
• I try to take care of everyone around me until I'm exhausted
• My breathing is shallow and I'm always tight in my shoulders
• I keep waiting for the other shoe to drop

- I don't tell friends my good news
- I numb out with food

Given what matters to me, what's an upgraded Story I could choose?
- My good life allows me to make my best contribution to the world

What are my actions and intentional practices that support that new Story?
- I breathe deeply and easily
- I move with confidence
- I see clearly what is and what isn't mine to do
- I share my rich life with others
- I mentor young people who are struggling
- I seek out partners for creative projects
- I am grateful every day
- I love my family and friends more deeply

The Right Boots for the Right Terrain

Whatever Story we're playing on the endless tape loop in our heads (and most of them are unconscious), it's there because at some point in our life it contributed to our survival. Danielle grew up in a family with an impatient father and three older brothers. Whenever she spoke her opinion, it was promptly met with ridicule. Sometimes she was even punished for being "stupid" or "impudent." It didn't take long for Danielle to learn to be extremely cautious about the way she behaved around her family. It was as if she wore soft shoes in all weather to keep silent, to avoid becoming a target.

When Danielle came to me as a client, she had just started a consulting practice but was fearful that she wouldn't be good enough to succeed. Meanwhile, her husband and children complained that she was controlling. She admitted to being a tyrant whenever she had a dinner party, insisting that everything be perfect: "That's not the way you set the table!" Her guests always enjoyed themselves, but her family sulked and retreated.

We began to expose the story that had shaped Danielle's life. What was the terrain for which she had needed quiet shoes? What was at the bottom of her feeling timid and trying to control and perfect everything? Both were characteristics that this very competent and likable woman did not want to continue. Toward the bottom of Danielle's pile of Stories we found: "I have to be beyond criticism." Together we explored what was fueling this story.

I asked, "What happened when you weren't flawless?"

"My father and brothers ridiculed and ignored me. I was dismissed. Most of the time I felt I was invisible to them."

It didn't take Danielle long to see that in order not to get pushed out of her family as a young girl, she had learned to be perfect: flawless and controlled. A wise choice, given her surroundings at the time—and given that the number one biological drive among human beings is to belong. Remember, our survival in early life absolutely depends on belonging to the tribe. Out on our own, we can't survive.

Danielle now saw how her strategy to achieve flawlessness had worked to keep her emotionally safe as a young girl, but she felt ashamed of her controlling behavior with her husband and children. The last thing she wanted was to alienate her family or to be uptight around her clients. The moment Danielle saw that her need to control was based on her need for safety, it was as if a gust of fresh air rushed into the room.

Every Story we tell ourselves exists because at some point it served a valid purpose. Danielle now relaxed and exhaled fully, probably for the first time in a long time. For decades she had remained vigilant, working to ensure she was beyond criticism. She had never allowed herself to go off duty! Her Story ensured that she felt left out. In that one moment of luxurious exhalation, she took up residence right in the middle of the circle of belonging!

The next step was to scan the story buffet for the upgraded Story that would feel best to Danielle. She left that session with five samples to try on.

- I belong!
- The universe celebrates my existence.
- God is thrilled with me. I can't do it wrong.
- All of my actions are inspired.
- I'm guided to do whatever is required.

No matter which story she chose, Danielle was going to come out a winner.

It's not necessary to peel away the layers until you find out why you have maintained loyalty to a particular Story. It may be helpful to do this, but it certainly isn't required. We're not trying to change the past. Rather, we're focused on creating a desirable future. Perhaps, like Danielle, you're quick to shame yourself for any trait or behavior that isn't exemplary (that's the Trance at work). Whatever Story you're responding to (*I have to be beyond criticism; I shouldn't make mistakes*) was a strategy originally designed to preserve your well-being. In its original context, it was brilliant. It fit the needs of its time. Now, as an adult, you're walking a new trail where different boots will serve you better. Thank your old Story as you step into your more spacious and empowering one.

Abundance is characterized by unrestricted flow, while contraction and fear squeezes that flow down to a trickle. **Contraction is the breeding ground of scarcity.** Be on the alert for places in your body where you're clamping down and refusing to allow yourself to receive. Your breathing (deep or shallow) is an excellent clue. Perhaps you're great at giving to others but you'll deprive yourself without a moment's hesitation. Are you being stingy with yourself? Sometimes, do you even feel proud of your ability to do without?

LAVISH	STINGY
(wholehearted)	(constricted, conflicted)
Taking risks	Not letting yourself dream
Laughing at yourself	Holding on to old guilt or shame
Being grateful	Always seeing what's missing
Savoring each moment	Living by the clock/no time for rest
Loving with abandon	Having a polite orgasm

Stinginess sits at one end of the continuum. At the other end is the experience of being lavish. For many of us, that word produces an instant response: *Oh, I couldn't, I shouldn't!* But if you don't give to yourself, how will your life become abundant? Lavish means stepping wholeheartedly into the big middle of life, rather than just tiptoeing partway in. Lavish means letting the flow of life move freely through you. Lavish isn't busy trying to control everything (that's stingy). Lavish is juicy, and yes, it's messy. It's alive.

If *stingy* and *lavish* sit at opposite ends of a continuum, where do you spend most of your time?

To choose better Stories, choose the language of *lavish*, of plenty, of flow. Danielle can now best be described as a juicy woman: confident, generous, playful, taking pleasure in her life. People continually report that they feel at ease and inspired around her. Now she doesn't work so hard, yet she enjoys greater success than ever, both at work and at home.

Changing Stories

Although we may be beginning to understand that our Story is just a Story and not the Truth, it still can feel a little risky to be tampering with it. Adaptive beings that we are, we've figured out how to tolerate the limiting story. We know our way around that territory, and we know what to expect from it. When we open ourselves up to a new possibility, a new Story, we often fear we're opening ourselves up to false hope. What if nothing changes? Then we will have to face disappointment which we could have avoided by sticking with the old Story. I agree that it's risky. It takes courage to move toward what you want, to come out of the cultural trance and wholeheartedly go after what matters to you.

· · · · · · ·

Transcendence is the only real alternative to extinction.

Vaclav Havel

· · · · · · ·

Changing Stories also means staying connected to your personal values and commitments. When Mick came to me as a client, he was filled with self-disgust because of his lack of success with his business. He was almost into his 60s, and the Trance had squeezed the juice of life right out of him. After a little digging, his default story "Life is unsafe" revealed itself. For years this story had prevented him from taking action, from believing in himself, from trusting others, and from attaining financial stability. If, indeed, life is unsafe, then one's attention needs to be on staying small and inconspicuous, out of danger, not carving out any clear identity. Mick wanted an upgrade, and he came up with "I can maintain my calm in the midst of anything." What do you think? Was it an upgrade? Or just another strategy to live inside his existing Story?

Mick saw it, too. The new story was just a more sophisticated strategy for dealing with life as though it were unsafe. His fundamental reality had not budged one inch. But then Mick did a remarkably wise thing: he stepped back and asked *Why does it even matter?* What was the big deal, anyway, about seeing that life was unsafe? Mick had a deep commitment to not passing on to his children the legacy of struggle-strain-skimp-suffer that he had adopted for so long. Because this legacy was important to him, he kept trying on new Stories until he found an upgrade that really worked. Here's the one he lives in now: "Great things just keep happening to me."

You'll note that Mick's new story doesn't really address the issue of life being unsafe. Instead, it is a new compass point on a whole new map. This reflects what Carl Jung suggested when he said that people don't actually solve problems; instead, their attention and energy move toward what is more compelling and the problem shrinks from lack of attention. When we orient our lives around what we most care about, we see new *ways of being* that we were blind to when we were focused on eradicating a problem. I invite you to refrain from attending to *something that needs to be fixed*. Instead, try looking at what you care about and what you really want.

The bottom line: It's All Story. Abundance is a Story. Scarcity is a Story. Yes, there are facts supporting both of them, but remember that it isn't the facts that shape our lives—it's our Stories.

Cooking Up a Tasty Reality

Two things create our reality: how we Orient ourselves (our Stories) and how we Inhabit ourselves (our lived experience). They are flip sides of the same coin. We design our Stories based on the shape of our experience, and, in turn, we shape ourselves around our Stories. In the next chapter we'll address how we Inhabit our Stories.

As we examine and transform our Stories, we get a chance to look at old patterns and, in the process, dredge up a few uncomfortable feelings. Doing this we can tend to get pretty serious, even glum. This is part of what makes self-development such a drudge. Ilana Rubenfeld, one of the pioneers of body-centered therapy, offers us the antidote. "Humor interrupts our trance of suffering and challenges the trio of fear, worry, and guilt." The more you can laugh at yourself, the easier the journey. Fortunately, there's no shortage of material.

You can make up any Story you want. Just ask yourself: What's the Story that supports what I most care about? Tell yourself that one!

PRACTICE
Upgrading Your Story
· · · ·

Take one of your default Stories and walk through the following steps using the examples on pages 39–40.

1. *What is one Story that just keeps playing, that parades across the bottom of the screen no matter what I'm looking at in life? What supports my taking myself outside of the Circle?* (Maybe it's a constant motto that you never actually say out loud or the bumper sticker that explains everything.) Dig a little deeper here. Keep asking yourself *Why?* and *What's behind that?*

2. *What are my current actions and behaviors perpetuating this Story?* What do you do? How do you breathe? Where do you hold tension? What gets your attention? What's your prevailing mood? What do you talk about or think about most of the time?

3. *Given what I care about, what are three to five upgraded Stories that would be useful?* You're not looking for opposites here; you're seeking out Stories that open new possibilities for you. You can't get this wrong, so go for it! Be lavish with yourself. The buffet is open.

4. *Which of these Stories appeals to me most?* Of your three to five Stories, choose the one that's most appealing to you, making sure it is stated in positive terms. Using the language of plenty, what would you say if you were in the Circle, feeling the flow of limitless Abundance? Remem-

ber: It doesn't have to be perfect the first time; you can always upgrade the Story later.

5. *What are the actions and intentional practices that will support this new Story?* Use the questions in Step Two with your new Story. Also, what do you want to add to your life so that you reinforce the new Story? Don't let it become a mere affirmation or a magic incantation. *Don't skip this part.* It transforms the Story from nice words into your lived experience!

6. Continue these new behaviors and practices until they are automatic for you.

7. Take another default Story and repeat this practice as often as you like.

· · · · · · ·

Banish the word struggle *from your attitude and your vocabulary.*

The Elders, Oraibi, Arizona Hopi Nation

· · · · · · ·

We break the Trance of Scarcity every time we interrupt the deeply inculcated messages we have been trained to accept as Truth and intentionally replace them with new, life-affirming Stories. Because we're all inextricably connected with each other, every time a Story in the vast human collection gets an upgrade it has has a positive impact on the quantum field—and that makes life a little better for everyone else.

Buckminster Fuller once said:

Something hit me very hard once, thinking about what one little man could do. Think of the Queen Mary—the whole ship goes by and then comes the rudder. And there's a tiny thing on the edge of the rudder called a trim-tab. It's a miniature rudder. Just moving that little trim-tab builds a low pressure that pulls the rudder around. And the rudder pulls the ship around. Takes almost no effort at all.

I like to think of each of us as Fuller's trim-tab. As each one of us makes a tiny correction, changing a tired old Trance Story into an empowering, life-affirming message, we can turn this world away from scarcity and toward the direction of plenty. Look out, Trance of Scarcity, we're onto you now!

Chapter 4

What We Embody, We Become

Our habits—which result from the Stories we tell ourselves—don't remain confined to our thoughts. Our Stories live in our muscles and in our nervous system until they become automatic. We shape ourselves around them, we embody their messages, and what we embody is who we are. When the ancient Greeks explored what constituted the ideal citizen, they identified four qualities: physically fit and strong, emotionally balanced and mature, mentally agile and alert, and having a spiritual or moral order. They saw that those qualities lived in the Soma—the embodiment of the self. Their exploration was an exercise in cultivating Soma, the self.

The Greek word *soma* refers to the living body in its wholeness—mind, body, and spirit as one. The principles of Somatics recognize that the self is indistinguishable from the body, from our lived experience. That's why Somatic practices are so effective; they retrain the nervous system by attending to the self as a whole. In this way, real change can take root and become lasting experience.

In our culture, talking about the body can be tricky because we link the body to appearance, fitness, and health, relegating it to the status of an object to be managed. The body is often considered an inert mass activated by something else, the mind or the spirit. For our purposes (embodying Abundance) we hold the notion of the body very differently: we see it as an intelligent, awake, and powerful part of an organic unity. To arrive at this understanding, we must investigate and mend the mind/body schism that disconnects us from ourselves and keeps us trapped in our heads, trying to win the battle of mind over matter.

. . . .

Mr. Duffy lived a short distance from his body.

James Joyce

. . . .

One profound cause of the schism between body and mind is that we have learned to mistrust or disregard our senses. We've lost touch with what poet Mary Oliver calls "the soft animal of your body." This numbness perpetuates our feeling of separation. Living as though we're disembodied (numb or disconnected), we lose touch with our self-direction, and we become extremely susceptible to the Trance of Scarcity. Rather than forge ahead with a firm sense of purpose, we're caught in the drift of whatever thought or action prevails; we go wherever we're led. We then become vulnerable to mind control. Think about it: Can you really separate yourself from your biology, your experience, your history? We are in-*formed* by our lived experience. It influences what we perceive and how we react to everything we encounter.

I grew up as a military kid. We lived a few hundred yards from the flight line and my days began and ended with the scream and quake of jets taking off. When our windows rattled, it was a sign to me that all was right with the world. Now as an adult, whenever the Blue Angels come to Seattle, I always make sure that when they fly over, I am close enough so my whole body thunders with the vibration. My system relishes the experience. Someone who has lived in a war zone would experience the sensation very differently.

If you went to a strict school where you were ridiculed for making mistakes, it's not likely that you are the first one to offer a new idea at work. If you grew up with lots of siblings and not quite enough food, you probably eat fast. If you have traveled internationally and adapted to constant change, chances are good that you feel energized in new settings rather than frightened. We are formed or shaped by our experience. That shape, or Soma, influences who we are. Like our Story, our Soma determines what is possible (and improbable) in our experience.

For a moment, slump in your chair, drop your chin to your chest, tighten your back and shoulders, make your breathing shallow, squint your eyes, and tighten your gut. Now get out there and be great! Lead that team, sell that project, host that event, attract that part-ner—you're a sure bet! It's absurd, right? We intrinsically know that this tight Soma we've crunched ourselves into is just not consistent with effectiveness. Even so, many of us are still living in some chronic variation of this shape, and we struggle all the harder because of it.

After decades of living, it feels as if our biology, neurology, and historical *ways of being* are converging to squelch our capacity to feel at home in the Circle. We've been practicing contraction for decades, holding a tension-filled Soma that makes ease and flow feel a long way off. When we begin to recognize how we have been shaped, we can also begin to change our *way of being* and reshape our selves to experience Abundance with ease. Embodied Abundance becomes our way of life.

The Body Is Not a Taxi for the Brain

Let's start where we all start, as babies. The work of Daniel Stern, MD, focuses on infant development. He has found that

> all mental acts are accompanied by input from the body, including internal sensations. The other input from the body includes all the things the body does or must do to permit, support, and amplify the ongoing mental activity, postures formed or held, movements of the eyes, head, or body, displacements of space, and contractions and relaxations of muscular tone.

The body and mind inform each other, and our resulting mental constructs create what Stern refers to as the *embodied mind*. The way we learned things in the beginning is how we continue to learn them: through the body-mind loop.

Our sensations are our earliest indicators of self and relatedness. In the very readable scientific book, *A General Theory of Love*, Drs. Lewis, Amini, and Lannon report that a full six months before an infant will be able to stand up on its own, that same infant can detect the most subtle changes in the emotional responsiveness of its caregivers. As human beings, as mammals, from our earliest moments we are seeking *limbic resonance*, "a symphony of mutual exchange and internal adaptation whereby two mammals become attuned to each other's inner states." We are masters at tuning in to those around us, bridging the gap between minds, assessing the nature and depth of our connection with others. All this crucial information comes to us through our senses, our Soma.

. . . .

Oh, for a life of sensations rather than thoughts.

John Keats

. . . .

When we lack such connection, our health and mental stability suffer. Even when a baby is given adequate food, without warmth, touch, and emotional connection the baby will die. We are *designed* to belong. Living outside the Circle in a Soma that is tight and armored puts us in a weakened state. Then, out of our desperate need to belong, we readily succumb to whatever Stories surround us. We adopt them so we can feel included, because inclusion equals survival. This is how the Trance of Scarcity takes hold. Once it inhabits our Soma, we remain stuck outside the Circle, trying in vain to wish our way back to belonging.

> When negative body states recur frequently, or when there is a sustained negative body state as happens in depression, the proportion of thoughts which are likely to be associated with negative situations does increase and the style and efficiency of reasoning suffers.

In this observation from his book *Descartes' Error*, neurologist Antonio Damasio confirms the mind-body loop and describes how we can step in and make changes, how we can self-observe and self-regulate so that we don't allow our "negative body state" to negatively affect our mental state as well. The process requires, first, that we be in touch with our own sensations.

Under stress, we tighten. Our bodily system contracts muscles, constricts blood vessels, alters breathing, and generally prepares for danger. It is designed to do so very efficiently for a brief period of time, and then to return to a more relaxed and fluid state. Sadly, what is meant to be a brief and intense organization of the human system has become a chronic *way of being* for many of us. Our muscles *stay* rigid and tight. We grind our teeth in our sleep. We're squeezed in and up, losing our sense of groundedness or flexibility. We're trapped in a conditioned reaction that perceives everything as more reason to bear down.

Without the Body, Never Mind

I'm not a fan of suffering or struggle. In fact, my life's work is devoted to interrupting struggle wherever I find it. As an educator and executive coach, seeing people stuck in Stories or Somas that strangle their aliveness launches me into action. I have witnessed myself and others valiantly trying to change our lives strictly within the mind-over-matter Cartesian model by conceptualizing, intellectualizing, rationalizing, and willing ourselves into a new reality. This method is insufficient, however, given our human nature. We are intricate psychobiological beings, not merely minds to be programmed with new data.

When I was first introduced to the discourses of Somatics about 15 years ago, I knew I had found the element that had been missing from all the well-intended work of personal and cultural transformation I had been involved with. I became an avid student and trained to become certified as a Master Somatic Coach. My teacher, Richard Strozzi-Heckler, has taken this important work to governments and corporations, consulting with such organizations as NATO and the Marine Corps. When I seek hope for the future, I take our cultural welcoming of Somatic principles as a very good sign. And in my own experience, I have found corporations, leaders, parents, entrepreneurs, and social leaders grateful for this powerful technology for personal and organizational change.

Heckler tells us:

> By living in our body we can generate a presence that has the power to allow genuine contact with our most inner core, with others, and with the environment. I have come to believe that by living close to our bodily and energetic processes, we may lead lives of increasing wholeness and purpose.

I've seen these changes, even in individuals and organizations for which exhaustion and defeat had gained what seemed like a permanent stronghold. By understanding our Soma and learning to listen to its messages, we become equipped to create a new reality.

. . . .

Knowledge is only a rumor until it's in the muscle.

New Guinea Proverb

. . . .

Thawing Out Our Life Force

Embodied Abundance is not about getting out of the way. It's about getting into the flow. We have already seen that muscular contraction is the ideal breeding ground for the Trance of Scarcity. Openness and relaxation, on the other hand, create the perfect incubator for Abundance. To become aware of our Somatic contraction or openness, we must become observers of a phenomenon most of us have been trained to ignore: the life of the body.

PRACTICE
Thawing Out
• • • •

While you're reading, *don't change a thing* about the way you are sitting. Just begin to observe. How would you describe your breathing? Is it shallow, full, tight, small, slow, fast? (This is no time for judging, just observe.) Let your attention scan through your body, starting at the top of your head. Scalp, face, eyes, jaw. Does it feel fluid or congested inside your skull? Throat, neck, shoulders—if you rated them (say one is relaxed and seven is tense), what number would you assign to each? Chest, back, arms, stomach. Do you feel movement, energy, dullness, discomfort, flexibility? Hips, organs, buttocks, genitals. Are they tight, relaxed? What do you notice? Legs, thighs, knees, calves, shins, feet, toes. Can you feel contact with the floor? Do some areas feel more alive than others?

The game here is to notice. The path to freedom begins with self-awareness, coming to know what is. Although we might want to race ahead to judge and categorize what we find, this actually precludes learning. And right now we're information gatherers. So just let yourself notice whatever you notice.

The language of sensation is new to many of us. You may not have words to describe what you find. You may not be able to locate any sensations to observe. Remember that we have been trained to dull down our senses and impulses, either to fit in or to tolerate our surroundings. Unfreezing all this takes both practice and a healthy measure of curiosity.

Embodiment is the result of what we practice. Sadly, most of us have been practicing various forms of contraction for many years. We learned early on to squeeze down our sensations, be they excitement ("People don't like little girls who are too loud") or distress ("If you keep crying, I'm going to have to put you down"). How open and alive can you be if your breath is high and shallow, your shoulders are tense, and your jaw is tightly clenched?

I perfected the clenched jaw decades ago. I've since learned that when I hold my jaw tight it determines how I interact with the world. Life becomes a series of hurdles to be conquered. Even if I'm not upset about anything, my tight jaw will lead me to feel *I've got to get this done* or *This is hard* or *I have to get through this.*

The good news is, now I know that one place I regularly contract is my jaw. As soon as I'm clenched, my day changes from a bright package of possibility to one huge, daunting To Do List. By continually checking in with what's happening in my Soma, I can catch my clenched jaw early and then I can relax it. I may have to relax it a dozen times throughout the day. But every time I do this, I'm interrupting an old pattern and replacing it with a new one. In the meantime, my day begins flowing much more smoothly.

. . . .

True learning, receiving the transmission of experience, happens at a level much deeper than cognition. It is in the experience of the lived body that we have the opportunity to contact and learn from the process of being alive.

Richard Strozzi-Heckler

. . . .

How do you get to Carnegie Hall? Practice, practice, practice. **We are always practicing something, and what we practice, we become.** In fact, the body is incapable of *not* practicing. Under stress, 99.9 percent of us will gravitate to our accustomed practices, our embodied *way of being*. David Morris, in his paper "Placebos, Pain and Belief," says that our biology, like our culture, limits the world we recognize and respond to. When we release the contraction in our bodies, our world expands too.

The Shape of Our Experience

How have you shaped or configured yourself in a way that is life-suppressing, that is not available to ease and flow, that squeezes down aliveness and keeps you out of the Circle? Yes, I'm flagrantly assuming that you have a habit of contraction, given that you're a member of a culture that for decades has lulled us to sleep with the Trance of Scarcity. What is the customized, highly sophisticated, well-practiced personal separation strategy that takes you out of the Circle? And once you're out, where do you go? You can find your suppressing practice by watching what is habitual (embodied) in how you operate.

It's Monday morning. Today is the day you present your team's new project to your boss and other executives. You stayed up late last night preparing. You need to drop your kids off at daycare on the way to work. The clothes you planned to wear are still at the cleaners. How do you move with all this: are you tight or at ease, hopeful or filled with dread?

Using the list below, note which traits or symptoms best describe your normal experience. Where on the continuum of Open to Contracted do you spend more time? What are the results you produce from there? What is your energy level like at the end of the day? What impact does that have on your interactions and relationships? On your self-esteem? What's the deeply embedded Story (masquerading as Truth) that lives in your Soma?

OPEN	CONTRACTED
ease	effort
prevailing trust	constant worry
relaxed body	chronic tension
effortless breathing	congestion
"can do" attitude	"can't happen" attitude
collaborative	competitive
curious, asking questions	judgmental, defensive
see opportunities	see obstacles
generous	withholding
willing to take risks	hyper-cautious
laugh easily at self	take self too seriously
energized	exhausted
fighting FOR	fighting AGAINST
resilient	resigned
grateful	keeping score
releasing things easily	hanging on
make clear requests and agreements	unspoken or vague expectations
generative, accountable	consumptive, "victim"
wholehearted	inner conflict

We pull ourselves out of the Circle so stealthily, it seems to confirm that we couldn't possibly belong there. When we live in contraction, the tension keeps us disturbed and attending to what's wrong. We think, *There must be a problem if I'm this tight and anxious.* Our body informs our thinking and our mood. If we consistently hang out in our physical tensions, we can actually become addicted to struggle; in an odd way, struggle becomes our comfort zone.

Many of us build our identity around making continued noble efforts in the face of almost certain defeat. We're in a cultural harness that says the way to be attractive is to look strong and hide our vulnerability. So we squeeze down a little tighter and separate ourselves a little more. Just look at a person's Soma, or shape. (We're talking about the shape of lived experience, not clothing size.) It's easy to see whether one lives inside or outside the Circle. The shape we inhabit over time becomes our outlook on life.

Our separation strategies are our Stories in action. Remember Mick who lived by the Story *Life is unsafe?* If something didn't happen as he hoped it would, he immediately moved into resignation. It didn't take any effort at all for him to go there—it was his default mode and he had been practicing it for years. You can imagine what the shape of resignation looks like: rounded shoulders, flaccid belly, crumpled chest, lips pursed, and eyes dull. As Mick shifted into his new orientation of *Great things just keep happening to me*, it was amazing to see how he changed his shape! He practiced a new shape, a new *way of being*, that included coming up to his full height, letting his shoulders rest back and down, breathing fully into the belly, feeling his feet solidly planted and his face relaxed and responsive.

We're not talking about body language or posture. Such terms refer to the body as an object, a thing we configure by putting arms this way and tilting the head that way for a certain effect. Shape is our lived experience; it reveals who we are. Maybe our parents knew something when they told us to stand up straight because it produced a different mood for us to live in than being hunched down or drawn back. While shape may reflect cultural differences, travel to any country and you can see who has a sense of freedom and self-direction and who does not, just by observing how they inhabit their Somas. A person raised in a position of authority is trained to take the shape of a leader or a sovereign. Such people are believable, coherent to themselves and those around them. They become the self that leads.

· · · · · · ·

As long as you do not live totally in the body,
you do not live totally in the Self.

B.K.S. Iyengar

· · · · · · ·

There's no question that we are formed and shaped by our history, whether that means never forgetting how to ride a bicycle or flinching at the sight of the family home we lived in 30 years ago. What we experience lives in our bodies and informs our actions and reactions daily. Wilhelm Reich, the Austrian psychoanalyst of the early 1900s, was among the first to recognize muscular armoring as a reaction to stress, either current or historical.

If you were yelled at frequently as a child, you might have developed protective muscular armoring in your neck and shoulders. Your eyes might be chronically squeezed. The yelling might have stopped decades ago, but if your muscles never got the message that they don't need to contract anymore, they're still on duty whether or not yelling is present. Just as in Danielle's story, the armoring you took on was absolutely the right choice at the time because it helped you take care of yourself. But based on who you are and what you want today, it may be time for a different shape.

Taking Off a Tight Shoe

Once something is embodied it becomes automatic, especially when we're under stress. This is both the good news and the bad news. We have been conditioned a certain way. Duane Elgin, in his book *Voluntary Simplicity*, suggests we would do well to acknowledge how much we act in preprogrammed ways. "We live ensnared in an automated, reflexive, and dreamlike reality," he writes, "that is a subtle and continuously changing blend of fantasy, inner dialogue, memory, planning, and so on." This dreamlike state is fertile ground for the Trance of Scarcity to take root.

Don't despair, however. We are not locked forever into the trances we have embodied. At the same time, I'm not here to blow sunshine by telling you that the whole process is a simple matter of relaxing your muscles and thinking happy thoughts. We must address things as they are, things we can count on.

One thing we can count on is that human nature is changeable. We are living beings, not inert clumps. We are made of live, malleable substances in constant flux. Dr. Amit Goswami, who wrote the textbook on quantum mechanics, confirms that "atoms are not things, they are tendencies."

So what does all this have to do with Abundance? When we recognize what creates our experience, we can change it. We can then respect, even revere, our human psychobiology, rather than ignoring it or trying to wish our way to a better life. Coming into a new relationship with embodiment, we become effective players in this game of plenty. Our awareness is our ace in the deck.

The person who wears a perpetual frown even when she is "relaxed"—how do you suppose that person sees the world? Or the one who inhabits a rigid back, tight arms, and hard eyes—what is she expecting life to deliver? If someone doesn't know that it's possible to inhabit life another way, she remains trapped in the Soma of the Trance of Scarcity. In contrast, the person who breathes deep and easy, who holds minimal tension in the shoulders, who lifts the heart and chest—she has a very different experience of life. The root of the word *courage* means *heart*. When we collapse the chest, we become easily dis-couraged, dis-heartened. When we fill our space and widen our chest, there is suddenly room for connection, purpose, and passion.

Our shape doesn't impact only us, it affects those around us. The shape we take on creates our identity, and others respond to us based on the shape they see. Remember, we humans are always deciding what everything means. All I need to do is look at you, and I create an instant story about you based on what I see; it's an automatic process. Just as an actor takes on a certain shape to get in character, we can experiment with how we inhabit ourselves until we find the Soma that best supports what we care about. We can choose to inhabit the shape that encourages the unrestricted flow of life—the Embodiment of Abundance.

Saying YES to the Flow

Thank goodness for great teachers! Our dog Tucker adopted us seven years ago, probably because she saw how much we needed to learn about real pleasure. The way she stalks a squirrel (which she has absolutely no intention of catching) is an exquisite act of choreography. Her muscles tremble with excitement, and she places each paw so slowly that the squirrel doesn't even notice she's moved closer. Her nose twitches as she draws in every scent, until her waiting explodes in a final burst of speed as she chases the squirrel up the tree, following it all the way to a second-tier branch. Then she proudly trots into the house, slurps up a loud, luscious drink of water, and paws the rug until it's just right as she walks the secret number of circles that make her ready to throw herself down with a satisfied sigh. In minutes she drifts into a contented asleep.

Tucker gives herself completely to the moment, just as Mihaly Csikszentmihalyi describes in his book *Flow*, a study in the state of high performance. In the state of flow, the moment is rewarding in and of itself. There is no split attention. This, I realized one day, is exactly the state that Tucker effortlessly inhabits. Whether she's tracking a squirrel or drinking water or preparing for a nap, she's completely in touch with her sensations and uses them to enhance her experience and her action. The more she feels, the more alive she is. And it gives her impeccable timing, with no action wasted.

I am fascinated by Tucker's unabashed experience of pleasure. My default mode has always been to settle for relief, instead. When I'm stressed or pushed or uncomfortable, relief sounds pretty good. At such times, I think that anywhere other than where I am would be preferable. But here's the problem: Relief takes me in the opposite direction from pleasure. Instead of becoming more alive, I move to being more numb. I move away from myself.

Erich Fromm identified *relief* as the satiation of deficiency, which he calls scarcity-pleasure, distinct from the abundance-pleasure of creation and growth. "We go to glut, relaxation, loss of tension," he said, "in contrast to the ecstasy, the serenity one experiences when functioning easily and at the peak of one's power. Relief is less stable or enduring than the pleasure that accompanies growth which can go on forever." Pleasure requires a certain degree of intimacy with ourselves. To be true to myself, I must know myself: what I enjoy, what I resist, what moves me. Pleasure asks that we reacquaint ourselves with who we are. It is through feeling sensations that we come to know ourselves in new ways. Our senses give us answers to questions such as *What do I feel? What calls me? How am I affected? What am I drawn toward? What do I avoid? When do I feel most alive?*

The more alive we feel, the more responsibility we have. This is only fitting because we have more *power* when we're fully alive. Instead of being the disembodied self that drifts away from life and goes numb, our embodied self's aliveness grants us greater discernment. As we become more self-aware and self-directed, our life force dramatically increases. When we are fully awake, our life force is more powerful than any trance.

So pleasure is a way of waking up! Who would have guessed it? Many of us have been taught that pleasure is the first step into the quagmire of sloth. But as Kay Redfield Jamieson asserts in her thoughtful book *Exuberance*, play is essential for human beings. She writes, "Play encourages fearlessness—that is, the readiness to explore one's world, test boundaries, reward flexibility and prepare one for the unpredictable." Time and space for play are, nevertheless, dwindling in our culture. Today's children have 40 percent less free time to play than they had 20 years ago. Some elementary schools have eliminated recess entirely, so students have more time to study for state-required competency tests. Such shortsightedness edges the body out of the picture and stymies our natural creativity, resilience, and excellence. Sadly, we end up with more Trance and less power.

PRACTICE
Flexing Your Pleasure Muscle
• • • •

To ensure that we don't go the way of the squeezed and disembodied, we take on practices that bring us to life.

1. At least three times a day, stop for a moment and scan your body for sensations, as described earlier in this chapter. You're an explorer traveling a new landscape, fascinated by everything you see. You don't waste a moment of your journey judging what you find. Your curiosity is boundless.

2. Without changing any conditions around you, how can you have more pleasure right in this moment? Make any adjustments in your Soma that allow you more ease and spaciousness (adjustments to breath and tension are always great places to start).

3. Inhabit yourself in your own version of my dog Tucker stalking her squirrel: fully present, fully alive. Notice your mood. Allow the colors and light around you to become more vivid. Feel your blood pumping, your breath moving, the sensations of your clothing against your skin. Be nowhere else but right here, right now.

4. Notice what happens to your experience. If you like the change, keep that shape.

Getting used to feeling sensations comes with—you guessed it—practice. But why even bother to feel more, since life is pretty challenging as it is? Well, simply put, the more sensation we can tolerate, the more present we can be. The more present we are, the more consciously we choose where to direct our attention and what action to take. The more choice, the more power. We get to own our lives, to climb out from the valley of habits we've been stuck in. Life can be messy, but it doesn't have to affect us as though a two-ton truck were barreling down upon us. We may still experience that kind of thing once in awhile, but we have options. We now know where our feet are, and we can move out of the way with purpose and grace. And in plenty of time.

Chapter 5

It's Not About Stuff, It's About State

Our primary premise in this book is that our experience of Abundance, of living in the world with effectiveness and ease, is determined by our inner state more than by our outer circumstances. We embody Abundance when we cultivate the state that matches ease and flow. So our focus is on state, not on getting our circumstances to line up neatly. Life is messy. Stuff happens, right? We stop wasting our time and energy trying to get life to behave because that's not where the leverage is. Anyway, who wants to work that hard?

We attend to our state because it creates our daily experience. Unless we're in a state that allows for ease, we're unable—literally incapable—of experiencing a life of ease and fulfillment. The dictionary defines *state* as *a mode or way of being*. As living beings we're always in a state of some kind or another: confusion, excitement, fatigue, hopefulness, calm, overwhelm, gratefulness, ambition, confidence, resignation, joy, curiosity. A person's state changes constantly in response to the stimulus of the moment. As a physician friend of mine says, "You want to be able to respond. If you lose that natural responsiveness, you're considered clinically dead." So we aren't trying to achieve a state in which we'll remain untouched or unmoved by life. Quite the contrary. We're seeking to increase our capacity for easy responsiveness, for aliveness and connection.

You and I have been focusing on getting to know, on a first-name basis, the two ingredients that create our reality and make up our state.

- **Our Stories—how we orient ourselves**
- **Our Somas—how we inhabit ourselves**

How we Inhabit and Orient ourselves allows for an open, flowing state of being or, conversely, for a contracted, stuck state of being. *Contracted* is crumpled and tight, squeezed down, tense, and armored. *Open* is at ease and relaxed, comfortable and spacious. When I contract or close down, I also separate myself. I move out and away from the very flow of life. In this condition, I begin to miss out on even the most obvious possibilities, ignoring a great deal of what's happening around me. When I expand or open, however, I come back into the Circle, merging with infinite possibility, and once again I become receptive to the flow.

. . . .

You carry all the ingredients to turn your existence into joy.
Mix them, mix them!

Hafiz

. . . .

What is the state that supports the experience of Abundance, of living in the world with ease? That's the state we want to cultivate so we can return to it quickly when we notice we've left it. We want to learn to stay within the state of Abundance so that we can not only sustain it, but expand it whenever we find ourselves in it. This isn't a rule book, now—you won't be graded on how you perform.

So as we continue in our exploration, don't put your state into a basket labeled Right or Wrong. This is not some kind of new take on how you should behave in order to be judged a "good person." The insightful writer, Anne Lamott, writes aptly of our common affliction. "Perfectionism is the voice of the oppressor, the enemy of the people. It will keep you cramped and insane your whole life." We want to learn to tolerate the messiness of life as well as our own imperfections, because doing so gives us profound access to life's juiciest secrets.

Fight, Flight, Freeze . . . or Flow

My partner, Tim, is a saint. In the 17 years we have been together, he has proven it time and again. I like to think of myself as helping him achieve sainthood by giving him lots of occasion for practice! Some would say that occasionally I get a wee bit wound up. (I'm really good at wrapping myself around my own axle.) I can tend to take myself just a tad too seriously. If you like a windstorm, I'm fun to watch. But even our dog Tucker leaves the room when I'm in that state, and all others enter cautiously.

When I am wound up to maximum torque, I need a release and I seek out a target. Who better than my beloved? In the early days of our relationship, this is how we did it: I would pounce and Tim would dive for cover. I would then escalate the situation by following him from room to room, closing off all avenues of escape. Words would be exchanged, a door would slam, the car would pull out of the driveway with both man and dog on board, and I would be left with myself as an audience of one. A few hours later Tim and Tucker would return, I would apologize, my apology would be accepted, and we'd be back to smooth sailing until the next windstorm hit and we started all over again.

It's been years now since I've reached full torque, but I can take very little of the credit for this change. First, Tim began to sit and listen to me as I railed. He cringed a little, but mostly he did a lot of deep breathing. Soon he was checking in with me at the first signs of my distress. Picture me stomping my foot, giving orders, interrupting his sentences. I'm speaking hypothetically, of course.

Then Tim got really sneaky. Whenever I was ensconced in some project, reeling toward a deadline, he began checking in with me. Did I want something to eat? Would I like to join him for a walk? Did I know how much he loved me? How was I feeling about my work, my writing, my schedule? He paid attention to how tight or relaxed my jaw seemed to be. Sneaky, very sneaky. Unbeknownst to me, Tim was monitoring my state and helping me adjust it before I even had a chance to get torqued up. He compassionately took it on because, at the time, I didn't seem to be able to do it for myself.

I'm a quick study, though. I started noticing when I was tight and strained and oh-so-ready-to-get-irritated. I even began noticing when I was simply humming right along, having a great time being creative. I began paying attention to how I contributed to each kind of state I got into. I noticed the shape I was holding and the Story I was following. I found that the more I noticed how my internal contents were tipping precariously, the quicker I could shift them back into a steady position. The circumstances—whatever was happening in the moment—actually had very little impact on the quality of the moment. It was the state I was in at the time that generated a cold front or a warm breeze.

Today Tim would tell you that I do the same thing for him, that I help him out of his own tough internal states and guide him out of harm's way. But of course he would say that. Like I told you, he's a saint.

Being able to recognize one's state is the first step toward shifting it. But shift it to what? (Answer: To the state that aligns with ease and flow.) Aligning with this state of Abundance, of ease and flow, is also known as Centering. Centering is most often associated with spiritual practice or with disciplines of the martial arts. Athletes practice Centering, performers practice it, parents practice it, and leaders practice it. Anyone who needs to be fully present in the moment, who wants to meet life's experience in useful and fulfilling ways, can benefit from practicing Centering. And for those of us intent on hanging out in the flow of Abundance and ease—for us, Centering is an essential ally.

Begin where you are. Attend to your current state. We tend to skip this part, leaping blindly toward wherever we think we should be. But there is gold to be mined from what we find in our habitual and automatic states. Just as I learned by watching my tight jaw, you'll begin to recognize your own early cues of tension or dis-comfort. Soon you'll have fine-tuned your observations about your internal state. You'll know what to watch for. As Yogi Berra once said, "You see a lot by observing." Don't skip this part.

Since we're malleable and changeable, we can make the shift to being open and centered. We can even make it permanent, freeing ourselves from the hold of automatic reactions and unwanted hab-its. This is how we break free of the Trance of Scarcity. Armed with a keen awareness of our internal state, we can remove whatever embodied tendencies are perpetuating scarcity and struggle in our lives. Once we've done that, we can replace self-sabotaging tendencies with consciously chosen practices that will align us with our natural state of fulfillment and ease, aka Abundance.

PRACTICE
Matching Your State to Ease and Flow
• • • •

Begin by standing. First **attend**, then **adjust**.

HOW YOU INHABIT YOURSELF

Attend. Bring your attention to your *physical sensations*. What do you notice about your breathing: is it full, shallow, high? What is the degree of tension or tightness in your muscles? How are you taking up your space: is your spine long and relaxed, or compressed and folded? Look for automatic behaviors such as clenching your jaw, holding your breath, jutting your chin, or wearing a permanent smile or furrowed brow. Scan your body for what you can observe. **Just notice**.

ADJUST

Breath: Bring your breath down so that it is riding low and full in your belly. Inhale and exhale completely. Let your stomach really move as you breathe. You may want to rest your palm on your belly so you can feel the movement there.

Weight: Let your weight rest in your hips, legs, and feet rather than holding it up in your shoulders or neck. Cooperate with gravity by letting your weight drop down. Your skeletal system is designed to hold you up without any strain from your muscles. Let go of all unnecessary tension.

Space: Fill out in length, width, and depth. Imagine lengthening down into the floor beneath you and up through the top of your head with no strain, just allowing the spine to be long and loose. Let your shoulders rest at your sides with room for your chest to breathe fully. Take a stance with your feet about hip distance apart. Explore taking a bit wider stance than you may be used to. This allows your hips and your back to relax, and it gives you a stronger base. Feel your feet on the floor. Now bring your attention to your back. (You may even want to put your hand on the small of the back to bring your awareness there.) See what you notice behind you, as well as in front of you.

HOW YOU ORIENT YOURSELF

Attend. Bring your attention to what kind of *thoughts* are active within you right now. Are you thinking in terms of judgments, concerns, or opinions; are you dwelling on events of the past or anticipating the future? What Story do you have about what is happening right now and what it means? Do you have *feelings* of connection or aloneness, confidence or anxiety, hope or resignation? What is your prevailing *mood* or outlook? What are you *belonging* to in this moment? **Just notice**.

ADJUST

Focus: Connect now to what you care about, to whatever matters most to you. Bring your attention to this moment; be present to what is happening here and now.

Mood: Choose the Story or attitude that is most useful, given what matters most to you. You have the power to decide in every moment how you engage with life.

Place: Remember that you *already belong* to the flow of Abundance, that you always have a place in the natural, effortless flow of the Circle. There is nothing you must do to earn eligibility. Only your consent is required.

No one is Centered or Open all the time, and that's not our goal anyway, so don't scold yourself when you find you're feeling off-balance. People who move easily through the world also move easily back into Openness when they find they've left it—and that's the goal. All of us have the capacity to experience this ease and freedom; we can **attend** and **adjust** our state as frequently as needed, and without judgment. Just noticing that you feel uneasy is an accomplishment, not a failure, because the act of noticing allows you to choose to move toward ease. So practice being attentive to your state, and practice not being offended or surprised that it is affected by what each new moment brings. Remember that being Centered doesn't mean being numb and impervious to life. Have confidence! When you know that you have control over what matters most—your state—you have the power to embrace life in all its fullness.

Moving from control to trust, living in the world with ease.

Be aware that most of the population doesn't know there is an option called Center. Most people have no Reset button. Because they live within the Trance of Scarcity, they are in fight, flight, or freeze mode all the time. From moment to moment, they're in a spiral of reacting, reacting, reacting—until the next thing happens and they react to that. They are worn out and worn down by the ragged energy of constant reaction.

Centering is about coming back to a state in which we remain aware of our power of choice, in which we can affect our life rather than merely suffer in reaction to events. No longer limited to the primal workings of our survival brain, we enter a state of higher functioning—one in which creativity, collaboration, and curiosity reside. We then gain access to our full capacity to be present in this world of unfolding moments. So please take a moment to appreciate the advantage you have, now that you've acquired the skill to shift your state even when others around you can't seem to do the same. Meet them with compassion rather than impatience. The more you stay centered in your responses to others, the better chance they will have of discovering a new *way of being* for themselves.

. . . .

Love is the only emotion that expands intelligence.

Humberto Maturana

. . . .

I guess you're onto me by now. You've probably already figured out that this practice of Centering and being Open is not the work of a couple of weeks. It's not even a matter of several months. It's a lifelong practice. The more you engage in it, the more completely it will serve you. The earlier you catch yourself in contraction and struggle, the quicker you notice the Trance of Scarcity taking hold of your jaw or your breath, the more readily you will be able shift to flow and ease. The game is to recognize the ways in which your experience of being Centered and Open is different from being off-center and contracted.

Say one day you're bopping along, feeling that everything's great, but as you check your state you notice you're holding your breath. You recognize that this is not what it feels like when you're Centered, so you relax your diaphragm and inhale deeply. As long as you're doing a state check, you might also tune in to your Story. At that moment you notice you're busy figuring out the future, so you stop to remember what matters most to you. You bring your attention back to the present moment. The shift doesn't have to show up dramatically, so watch for the smallest cues. The general rule of thumb is this: We're off-center or contracted whenever we're not fully present to flow and ease.

Gradually our experience of state-attending and state-adjusting becomes more and more subtle. It is said that the founder of Aikido, Morihei Ueshiba, always appeared to be completely Centered. When his students asked how he did it, he replied that he was often off-center but that he simply noticed that fact and returned to Center quickly, before others even realized that he was off. The more awake we become to the nuances of our inner state, the more quickly and easily we can adjust it.

He Didn't Call . . . Again

The day I sat by the phone waiting for that guy in high school to call (Remember him? He disappointed me back in Chapter 2), I didn't have any awareness of my state or how to adjust it. I was completely at the mercy of my own perception of the circumstances. Hunker down and get through it was about the best option I knew. Looking back, I can still feel how miserable it was, how crushing, how devastating. Bless my wise brother for interjecting a little factual reality into my world!

Hearing my brother's words in that moment shifted my state immediately. I wasn't aware of this connection at the time, I just figured life had relented and stopped punishing me for a moment. I was still completely enslaved by what had happened to me, not yet realizing that I was the one creating my experience. I would love to tell you I learned my lesson right then and there, and never had any subsequent need for a review. But if that were so, I wouldn't have this generous supply of tales to tell on myself, and that's the least I can do.

Fast forward 30 years. It's after my divorce and I am once again seeking the knight who will rescue me. Once again I have chosen poorly. I am utterly devoted to the Trance of Scarcity; whatever it dictates, I'll do. Even though Buzz, my knight *du jour*, was articulate, handsome, charming, and liked dogs, he was your basic noncommittal male. Monogamy was nowhere in his vocabulary or his game book.

We had been dating for a few months. I use the term *dating* entirely euphemistically, because basically I was available whenever he called. One day I worked up my nerve to speak to him about my preference that he not see other women. He listened patronizingly as I made my case. Then he verbally patted me on the head and reassured me that I was welcome to have any preference I wanted, but that he had no intention of changing his MO.

"I'm not being unreasonable. I just want to be happy!" I wailed.

And then, get this, here's what he said: "Then go ahead and be happy. I'm not stopping you."

This time the lightening bolt of wisdom illuminated the whole sky of my mind. I got it. My happiness was not up to him. What great news! It was all up to me. My satisfaction wasn't going to be the result of all the conditions being right. It wasn't dependent on my partner or the lack of a partner. My happiness was mine to design; I was the keeper of the magic ingredients. The potion was in my possession!

Since I was raised with excellent manners, a year later I wrote Buzz a heartfelt thank you note for helping me to see all this. He didn't answer, but it didn't matter. He always thought he was God's gift to women—and in this particular case, he certainly was to me.

Easing into Ease

Most of us like the feeling of being in control. We think that if we keep our hand on the lever, things will go just the way we want them to; we'll be satisfied. The problem with always having to be in control is that you have to stay at the control panel. You can't leave to get out on the dance floor. The indomitable Katherine Hepburn knew this. She said, "If you follow all the rules, you miss all the fun." It's true even when you yourself are the rule-maker.

Living in the world with ease, embodying Abundance, means moving from control to trust. It's a lot to ask of yourself. So take care that you don't get moralistic with yourself and try to *force* yourself to "Quit controlling and move over to trust right this instant, young lady!" It's something we learn to ease in to; it's great to try it on in small doses first. Try releasing the control-contraction by 2 percent, 5 percent, 8.3 percent, a little at a time. Then watch what happens. You can always tighten up again.

Remember that you've been keeping yourself contracted for a while now; you have history with your contraction. It felt safe, it was smart, and it was easier to live that way at various times and for various reasons. To find out if that contraction is still useful to you today, ask yourself, "What do I most care about? What matters to me deeply?" Check to see whether your state works in service of your deepest commitments and values, or if it precludes them.

Diana, a student in one of my *Embodied Abundance* telecourses, happily shared her story with the group.

> One of my foundational realities is perceiving life as a struggle. I perceive that people are out to get in my way. I drag myself to and through everyday chores like grocery shopping and washing dishes. Then one day Victoria asked me, "What if you let it be as easy as it wants to be?" *Wham!* I realized that, as a result of my recent forays into Somatic understandings of trauma and conditioned tendencies, I had set myself up to believe that changing those tendencies and habits would be a long and difficult project!
>
> Since hearing that question, I find myself constantly asking it, especially in the face of something I find challenging, difficult, time-consuming, or nearly impossible. That question instantly puts me back into the flow. I get a sense of support and Abundance, which allows me to be more open, playful, curious, and ready to receive.
>
> There's a strong feeling of momentum in my life now, largely without a sense of urgency. I'm enjoying the present more and more, even when I wish to change it dramatically. I'm delighted to say that I now spend the better part of my daily life in an appreciative, abundant place.

· · · · · · ·

We are not creatures of circumstances,
we are creators of circumstances.

Benjamin Disraeli

· · · · · · ·

Thawing out from the frozen state of control can be messy, and it can certainly feel uncomfortable. If you've been out hiking or skiing when it's really cold, your hands or feet may get a little numb. As they begin to thaw, it doesn't necessarily feel very good. But that doesn't mean you want them to stay numb. It's worth the temporary discomfort to have working appendages again.

Years ago someone told me, "When we come unglued, we get unstuck." At the time I felt very much as though I had already been completely disassembled, so it didn't really scare me. I had already come unglued. But hearing this helped me to stay a tiny bit more open to the ungluing, because I was definitely in favor of getting unstuck in my habitual patterns. And sure enough, many of those patterns got dissolved in the process.

Please remember this: Whatever you're asking of yourself—check to be sure that it's in service of what matters most to you (not what someone else says should matter to you). It sounds like this:

> *On behalf of being more loving, on behalf of having a successful business, on behalf of being a great parent, on behalf of fully inhabiting my life, I'm willing to tolerate temporary disruption and discomfort, because I now know that staying closed and tight can't take me there.*

PRACTICE
Matching Your State to Ease and Flow
••••

1. Check your state. Here is the senior practice in the experience of Abundance. Hold this activity as a basic function, part of being human—you brush your teeth, you put on your shoes, you check your state. In time it will become so habitual that you won't be able to imagine going through a day without doing multiple checks on your state.
2. At least five times a day (more is better): Stop. Attend to your current state and adjust to the state of being Centered and Open. Follow the steps listed above for Cultivating Your State.

3. Watch for the smallest clues to when contraction or separation is taking place. The more you look, the more you can find. Assume there is always one more.

4. Stay awake and curious, never judging what you find. When you find a tough spot or want to pull away, be tender with yourself.

5. Remember why it matters to you.

6. Don't stop.

My mother spent the last years of her life in the snare of Alzheimer's. As her disease progressed, being with my mother became increasingly heartbreaking. After a visit with her, I'd often sit in my car and sob. How could this be happening to my mother? What purpose could her suffering possibly serve? I was outraged, angry, resentful, and deeply sad.

What was most important to me and my brother was for my mother to be comfortable. We wanted her to know she was loved. Every time I went to see her, I first attended and adjusted my state again and again, until I was satisfied that I was Centered and present before going in to see her. Often I had to walk around in the parking lot for a few minutes to accomplish this. I was committed to protecting my mother from the spew of my distress about her disease. It meant spending a lot of time bringing my breath down into my belly. Relaxing the tightness in my forehead and throat. Bringing my attention to my love for her and peeling the bony fingers of despair off my heart. Because I knew what being Centered and Open felt like, I knew where to look for contraction. When at last I was satisfied that I was really embodying flow and openness, I would enter her room.

My times with my mother were wrenchingly precious. As she lost her capacity for language, eventually all that was left was just being together. Sometimes I would talk or sing to her, but often we just sat together holding hands. What I had to offer her was my presence, my full availability to be touched by the moment, entirely without armor. Those visits with her became a kind of sanctuary for me, away from all the time pressures and demands of daily life. I was simply there with my mother, being present with things as they were. My mother's final gift to me was helping me see that remaining Open, whether to grief or delight, allows us to be fully alive. Out of love for my mother, I learned to meet my discomfort and allow it to settle into the state of Centeredness. And I am all the richer for it.

Cultivating the state of ease and flow is not something you do just for personal reward, though it is deeply rewarding. Boomeritis, a term coined by Ken Wilber, can undermine our place in the Circle; it amounts to an "unusual dose of self-absorption and narcissism." It may seem that attending to getting your life in order is a worthy enough investment of your life energy. But it's not big enough for your spirit. When you're living and moving in the flow, your capacity to love, to contribute, to receive, to inspire, to comfort, and to rise to the occasion expands exponentially. You merge your greatness with that which is greater than yourself. Doing so, you begin to exert a vital impact on the world around you.

Aliveness Welcome Here

I was born and raised in the South, and I appreciate books by and about Southern women. We're a sometimes peculiar breed, one for which I make no apology. One of my favorite such books is *The Divine Secrets of the Ya-Ya Sisterhood*, an excellent chronicle of learning how to lean into life rather than keeping it at a safe distance.

The protagonist, Sidda, takes us through her mother's life and her own, complete with all their struggles and longings and misunderstandings, all the years of "charm hiding fear." At the end of the book, Sidda reconciles with her mother and reflects on her life. "I have been missing the point," she says. "The point is not knowing another person, or learning to love another person. The point is simply this: *How tender can we bear to be?*"

Being open to the flow of Abundance will not eliminate pain from your life. It won't instantly make you wealthy. It won't even guarantee that people will come to your parties. What it will do is reinstate you at the center of your own life. Being open to the flow of Abundance will sustain your capacity to greet whatever comes your way, as you dare to be enriched by it.

·······

We have arrived at the end of Part I of our exploration. You now have the necessary equipment to create the reality of your choice. We've dispelled misconceptions, identified Trances, laughed at ourselves (or at least at me), and taken up residence at the center of our own lives.

If you like, you may stop right here, because you're now in possession of the secret formula that most people are missing. If you do these practices consistently, your life is going to feel very different to you. Not only that, people are going to start asking you what you're up to. So let 'em have it, straight up! Spread the wealth.

In Part II we'll be making our way around the Cycle of Abundance. To make this next part of our journey most worthwhile, you will need to be actively engaged in the practices presented in Part I. Just as people absorbed in the Trance of Scarcity have particular habits and ways of being, people who live in Abundance also practice particular behaviors and ways of being. These practices result in deeper pleasure, ease, belonging, and ongoing expansion in our lives. We'll be getting to know those life-changing practices even more intimately, so that they permeate our experience, radiating outward to others as well, with increasing benefit all around.

PART II

FLOW

*It's not about getting out of the way;
it's about getting into the flow.*

6

Chapter

The Cycle of Abundance: The Six Phases of the Flow

I had been gleefully riding on the gravy train of consulting gigs. I was halfway through a two-year contract providing leadership development to upper managers for a big corporate client on the East Coast. It was the early '90s, business travel was easy, and the work made it worth flying across the country every other week. I was happy with the client, the work, and the steady income. And they were happy with my work, or so I thought—until the call came.

"Our new CFO has cancelled all external consultants effective immediately."

With both hands, I steered the shaking phone back to the receiver. In one phone call I had lost over $70,000. The floor disappeared as a black hand began to close around me; its bony fingers squeezed until breathing became nearly impossible.

Not only had income disappeared, but I had done what a consultant must never do—I had stopped marketing and cultivating potential clients.

An hour passed, maybe more. Another day went by, maybe more. At some point it occurred to me that staying in bed eating carbohydrates nonstop was probably not going to save me from joblessness. I forced myself to get dressed and shuffled into my office prepared to face the empty calendar. The bony fist was still clutching my chest; I was getting used to its grip. Inside I was gasping, and outside it was raining. Hard.

Soon I was hunched over my desk like a jeweler with failing eyesight, placing call after desperate call, begging various former clients for work. After four consecutive cloudy days of dialing, I had experienced over 30 different versions of the same conversation: no one had any leads to offer me, but they wished me the very best.

The fifth day was sunny and clear. Again I was stationed at my desk, phone in hand. Our dog Ginger padded over and laid her head on my leg, indicating that she wanted to go out. I let her outside, leaving the door open so she could come and go. A few minutes later, Ginger's head was once again on my knee. I stopped to rub her head and looked at her. Her almond eyes were alive with fun and soft with pity. Ginger wasn't going to take no for an answer. I sighed, unchained myself from the desk, and headed outside with her. It was a crisp fall day. Billowy clouds floated through the bright blue sky on a light breeze that was making the leaves dance.

Even in my obsessive state, I couldn't help noticing how beautiful it all was. For the first time in days, I let myself stretch and take a breath. Ginger assumed her "bet you can't get me" posture, and in no time we were wrestling and snuggling on the plush lawn. My back unfurled against the sturdy earth. The urgency subsided. Gradually the fist that had been clutching at my chest began to loosen. I forgot about being jobless and became absorbed in the brilliant sky. It was the blue of afternoon football games, of high-in-the-mountains camping; the blue of floating down a narrow river in a kayak. A rich succession of memories inserted their snapshots into my mind's eye.

I so loved that particular shade of blue. I had taken a watercolor painting course a year earlier, in which I had learned to really see the different hues of each color. Thinking of the course reminded me that I had recently offered to loan my friend Kathy a video demonstrating my watercolor instructor's method. I decided to make a quick call to her before getting back to the Goliath task of finding work.

"Hi Kathy, it's Victoria."

"Oh my gosh, I don't believe it! I was just talking about you yesterday. Are you in town for awhile?"

"Yes, my schedule actually just . . . "

"You're kidding. This is too good to be true! I just got a huge promotion as VP of Product Development and I've got to get my team in shape fast. You're exactly who I need, but I figured you were unavailable because of your big contract. Do you have *any* room in your schedule? I'll take whatever you can give us. *Please say yes!*"

The fist around my chest went suddenly limp, and I heard myself fully exhale for the first time in days. Suddenly here was a sweet slice of work served up to me all on its own, completely unrelated to the desperate phone calls I had been making. It was as though the work had found me. And all I had done was go outside and look at the sky.

That shift was crucial, however. It had taken my attention and energy *away* from lack and struggle. Up until that moment, I had been so consumed with how hard it was going to be to find work that I didn't dare waste a minute looking at all the options or even considering that it could be easy. I was in panic mode, my whole system organizing itself as though I were under siege. The fist that had been clutching my chest was my own. It wasn't until Ginger invited me outside (where I began to see and appreciate color again) that I thought of calling Kathy, which led me straight to a golden opportunity just waiting for me to arrive and scoop it up.

My circumstances hadn't changed, but my relationship to them had shifted dramatically. When my state shifted from tight and terrified to relaxed, playful, and receptive, a new world appeared—because I was at last available to see it. It was a graphic illustration to me that our experience of Abundance is always a function of our state. While placing those worried, fearful phone calls, my state had contracted down to a nub. I wasn't in the Circle or the flow; I was completely mired in the Trance of Scarcity's web: *figure it out, hurry, this is urgent, you're running out of people to call, you're doomed.* That state of contraction kills intuition and inspiration.

. . . .

Even if you live to be 100, it's really a very short time.
So why not spend it undergoing the process of evolution,
of opening your mind and heart, connecting with your true
nature—rather than getting better and better at fixing,
grasping, freezing, closing down?

Pema Chödron

. . . .

Here is a brief introduction to the Cycle of Abundance and how it flows in all its six phases. We often think of Abundance as being like a river: flowing but moving only in one direction. That image is misleading because Abundance is much smarter than that. Abundance renews and replenishes itself, flowing in a circular pattern the same way the breath moves: first the inhale and then the exhale. Each part of the cycle naturally makes way for the next.

We'll go around clockwise for a quick look at the signs of each phase as it's embodied, and we'll also look at symptoms of operating from the Trance of Scarcity. In the following chapters we'll explore in depth how it looks and feels to embody each of the six phases of the cycle. You'll learn specific practices for embodying Abundance, so that ease and plenty begin to emanate from you as naturally as your breath.

ALIGNING

• • • •

Forcing, the opposite of Aligning, demands that we figure it out and make it happen all by ourselves before disaster strikes.

When we're Aligning, we recognize that we already belong in the Circle. We move with the flow, awake to inspiration and opportunity. We relinquish the burden of being the "solitary enforcer" and instead merge with the workings of an intelligent universe already at work on our behalf, creating opportunities and resources beyond our imagining (like Kathy and her new team, who needed my services).

Signs of Embodied Aligning include ease, pleasure, aliveness, and relief.

ATTRACTING

• • • •

Grasping, the opposite of Attracting, relies on strain, push, and worry as our only hope to avert disaster.

Attracting is energy that is focused yet unforced. By directing our energy and expectation (how we Inhabit and Orient ourselves), we are not *making* anything happen. We are, rather, drawing toward us what we want as though we held a magnet. The more wholehearted and peaceful we are about what we want, the more irresistible we are to it. Once I had consciously replaced my Story that getting *work is hard* with a new Story that *great work finds me*, work began coming to me steadily, with effortless ease.

Signs of Embodied Attracting include ease, pleasure, aliveness, and confidence.

RECEIVING

• • • •

Numbing, the opposite of Receiving, closes down our aliveness and keeps us remote and unsatisfied. The less we feel, the safer we believe we are.

Receiving means being available in the fullest sense of the word—allowing the precious moments of life to touch us deeply. Receiving has nothing to do with being worthy, but it has everything to do with being Open. Receiving is the depth of inhalation. If I had been Numb, the most that Kathy's offer could have brought me was relief. But I welcomed the offer fully and allowed it to dissolve the wall I had been constructing around myself. Everything became richer for me that day. I woke up to the blessings already present in my life, including one very sweet, persistent, and patient dog.

Signs of Embodied Receiving include ease, pleasure, aliveness, and satisfaction.

GRATITUDE

• • • •

Arrogance, the opposite of Gratitude, keeps us armored so that we stay focused on what's missing and why we should be envious and disapproving.

If we receive fully, Gratitude follows naturally. Gratitude is generative energy that acknowledges our connectedness. Gratitude deepens the pleasure of Receiving and makes us eager to accept more and more good things into our lives. When I received Kathy's offer, I instantly became inspired about the help I could offer to her team, and my work with them turned out to be more innovative and effective than they had even dreamed. They gratefully referred me two new clients who were equally delighted with what I had to offer.

Signs of Embodied Gratitude include ease, pleasure, aliveness, and joy.

GENEROSITY

• • • •

Hoarding, the opposite of Generosity, is a lonely game of me-mine, which demands stockpiling and leaves us distrustful and isolated.

When we are full, sharing comes naturally. Generous souls know they cannot be diminished by Giving—the more they share, the fuller they feel. What they have, they want others to have. Generosity recognizes our interconnectedness, our mutuality, our oneness. My consulting work with Kathy's team revealed additional needs within her organization, for which I recommended other consultants. I was able to share the work I had been given, and everybody won.

Signs of Embodied Generosity include ease, pleasure, aliveness, and resilience.

GIVING

• • • •

Stagnation, the opposite of Giving, requires that we constantly keep our shields up, careful not to let anything go. It's the quickest route to impoverishing ourselves.

When one gives from an open and full heart, Giving is pure pleasure. It's a creative and spontaneous act, never an obligation. Giving is the exhalation that makes room for the next inhalation. I made the call to Kathy for the purpose of giving her something, the painting instructor's video that I had mentioned in passing. It was an act without strings or expectations, yet in less than a minute it resulted in a contact that enriched my life beyond my wildest dreams, in a flow that continues to this day.

Signs of Embodied Giving include ease, pleasure, aliveness, and expansion.

·······

*The winds of grace are always blowing. But we must
raise our sails.*

Ramakrishna

·······

In the story above, what led to my shift of state? I finally *relaxed*. Do not underestimate how potent relaxation can be! Just ask the Olympic skier as he begins his slalom, or the diamond cutter as drill meets stone, or the heart surgeon deftly repairing an artery. Relaxation fosters focus, precision, fluidity, and flawless timing. When I'm relaxed, my psychobiology makes the most efficient use of my blood flow, hormone release, oxygen transfer, and nerve impulses. The Latin root of the word *relax* means *to loosen*. (A good move when one is engaged in strangling oneself!)

Contraction, in contrast, is the perfect breeding ground for scarcity. It keeps us on guard and hunkered down, believing that the more tightly we're wound, the better. And the tighter we get, the more panicked we become. By letting my muscles and breathing relax, all manner of fresh life energy was suddenly free to move once again. Once it started moving, I could entertain different perspectives about myself and my life. I was a new person looking through a new lens. In this way, Story and Soma work together in concert. You can make your shift by changing either one—it doesn't matter which takes the lead.

Let me repeat: My circumstances didn't change. Kathy had decided she wanted me to work with her team before I ever called. The opportunity was there all along, but my attention was directed elsewhere. All my energy was focused on frenzied attempts to stave off doom.

By turning my attention and energy away from Forcing things to happen, to being available to the gifts already available all around me (the beauty of the sky, the love of my dog, the joy of moving and breathing in the crisp fall air), I allowed those ambassadors of Abundance to usher me into the flow of inspiration and opportunity. Once Aligned, I naturally followed the spontaneous impulse to call Kathy—not to ask for anything, but *to give her something*— and the surprising and delightful result was one I could never have forced. Kathy met my gift with one of her own: a bit of welcome work that happened to be just what I needed at that moment.

Flow, Flow, Flow Your State

The natural state of Abundance is flow, endless and interconnected. All the way to the bone, that flow was accessible to me. Once I began following the flow, it led me on a playful route to Abundance.

The dog bone was connected to the play bone
  The play bone was connected to the outdoor bone
    The outdoor bone was connected to the sky bone
      The sky bone was connected to the color bone
      The color bone was connected to the painting class bone
    The painting class bone was connected to the Kathy bone
  The Kathy bone was connected to the telephone bone
    which was connected to the "I just got a promotion and I
      need you" bone
    which was connected to the "I have the skills to help you" bone
  which was connected to the ability-to-provide-great-value bone
    which was connected to the new work bone
      which was connected to the Cycle of Abundance bone!

A flawless structure! Flow is constant, creative, intricately woven, and multifaceted, not limited by the small range of our imagination.

We don't have to supervise it, control it, or entice it; our role is simply to let the flow do what it naturally does—move in freedom. We allow flow its freedom of movement by removing whatever artificial barriers we have in place.

Fortunately, our biology gives us definite clues about how embodying Abundance looks. The heart, although it never takes a vacation, is at rest more than it is in action. With use our muscles get strong; with overuse they become sore and weak. Observe the breath, that wonderful involuntary reflex that ushers oxygen in and out of the body; it serves as a perfect model of the flow of Abundance.

Take a moment to check this out for yourself. Exhale completely. Then do nothing, and watch what happens. Your body will let you know when it's time to breathe, and it will do so quite efficiently. You will spontaneously pull air into your lungs. When that happens, again do nothing. Sure enough, soon your body will just as readily release the air. Ride along with your natural breathing pattern for a minute, and just observe. What is the regular rhythm of your breath when you're not forcing it? Fluid or staccato, easy or forced, efficient or wasteful? Just notice.

Now try this exercise again. But this time, make sure you remain consciously in charge. Exhale, count to 20, then take in a tiny bit of breath through your nose, and hold it in. Count to 10, then exhale that breath. Count to 10, and repeat the pattern. Breathing isn't very efficient or pleasant that way, is it? It's awkward trying to regiment what is naturally fluid and seamless. Inhaling and exhaling are inextricably linked, and the whole process works best when inhale and exhale are allowed to flow into and from each other without mental interference (such as a Story of scarcity).

When you open to the flow, Abundance is all around you. It can take the form of an art class that leads to a great job two years later, a delayed plane flight that results in meeting a new love, an article in the newspaper that inspires a new product idea. Abundance draws on anything and everything, not just what you're able to conjure by yourself.

That's why Abundance can flow freely—because it replenishes itself at every turn. The Cycle of Abundance is identical to the cycle and flow of life energy. That energy includes but is not limited to money, relationships, health, inspiration, opportunity, and self-expression. The more clear and free-flowing your breath, your muscles, your attention, and your thoughts, the greater the flow of Abundance in your life. So who plays the role of the restrictor? You guessed it: you do.

Aligning
and Attracting

Letting things be as easy as they want to be is a skill in itself. My friend Jerilyn is a culinary consultant who designs exquisite recipes for restaurants and food corporations. Her way of finding the perfect ingredients for her recipes is part science and part Alignment.

After she does batches of tests to close in on the right formula, Jerilyn stops. She does this on purpose. She just drops everything and goes for a walk in nature or works in her garden. *But she's got a deadline!* says the Trance of Scarcity. *Shouldn't she be working on the new product?* Well, she is. By resting into the flow and distancing herself from any inclination to force, the right combination reveals itself and she is right there to receive it. Then she walks back into the house, tests the recipe, it's a hit, and her client is delighted beyond expectation. Jerilyn has repeated this miracle many times. She makes it look easy because she doesn't make it hard.

While wrestling with a problem, Albert Einstein was known to take a break and play the piano or violin, then stop and shout, "I've got it!"

Aligning: Effortless Ease

When we rejoin the Circle, accepting our innate belonging, opening ourselves to the flow, merging with that which is greater than ourselves and trusting that it is operating on our behalf in marvelous unseen ways, then quite naturally we are moved to inspired action rather than frantic muddling. Aligning calls for a shift in Story and in Soma—a change in the way we embody (in our muscles and tissue and nervous system) what we believe to be true about ourselves and our lives. Energy follows Attention.

When we operate from the stance of Forcing (the opposite of Aligning), we are run by what is external to us. As Lynne Twist says, we live in a prevailing sense of inadequacy about life. As victims of a merciless world, we must fight back to make the world behave like it should. We take everything personally: traffic, leaky pens, how far we have to park from the door, the fact that other people take up space. In that state we begin on empty, demanding that something else, someone else fill us up. We're like the man who looks at his woodstove and bargains, "First make me warm, and then I'll give you wood."

Americans work more of the time than any nation in the world, an average of nine weeks a year more than Europeans do. That's an entire summer's difference! The American vacation becomes a scant week for flopping down on the beach, sleeping for the first two days, then cramming in every possible recreational experience (which often includes overeating and drinking too much), and then starting to panic about getting back to the job to take care of business. How many people do you know who fit the workaholic profile?

Work has its place, of course. I love my work; it feels like play to me. Work is a wonderful expression of our creativity, our contribution. But too often we have turned our work into an endurance game of straining and forcing. This applies to earning money, working to maintain a loving relationship, or opening the business you always wanted to start. Suddenly livelihood is no longer about what you produce, but how damned hard you worked for it! The more burned out you feel, the greater the evidence that you've earned it.

Poppycock! How hard you work has no correlation to how much you can have. In the Cycle of Abundance, that's just bad math. There is nothing wimpy about drawing on the resources of Something greater than yourself. In fact, that's precisely what the most creative people in the world have done for centuries. They hop on their inner tubes and join the obvious flow, instead of rowing upstream through some backwater bog. The better part of their brilliance is in noticing the flow and jumping right in.

Aligning   *Forcing*

Would you like a life of ease and joy, love and fulfillment? Align with all that is already flowing toward you. Go ahead; it has your name on it. Making yourself available is the key to Aligning.

· · · · · · ·

Genius means little more than the faculty of perceiving in an inhabitual way.

William James

· · · · · · ·

Years ago, some friends of mine shared the formula called HALT. It stands for Hungry, Angry, Lonely, Tired; and the advice was *Don't make decisions or put yourself in vulnerable situations when you are any of the above.* Why? Because you're not in the best state to choose in that moment, and making choices from the wrong state often leads to difficulty and disappointment.

Contraction, and with it the inclination to Force rather than Align, comes in many forms. Be on the alert for the smell of contraction. At the first whiff, wake up from the Trance and step into the Circle. Some common signs of the Trance are:
- You're anxious about the big day ahead of you.
- You're dreading a tough conversation.
- You're feeling cranky, impatient, and judgmental.
- You're panicking about a big decision.
- You have just scared yourself while looking at your bank balance.
- You feel lonely in your relationship.
- You're driving and you're in a hurry.
- You're awake at three in the morning worrying about tomorrow.
- You keep revisiting an old resentment or humiliation.
- You're determined to have quality time with your kids no matter what.

Aligning doesn't keep life from being messy, it just keeps the mess from becoming a permanent stain. Life will do what it does. But nothing it does has the power to limit your world of possibilities.

· · · · · · ·

All things are inventions of holiness. Some more rascally than others.

Mary Oliver

· · · · · · ·

Smarter, Sweeter, Sexier

There are many practices that Align us with the flow. They include meditation, tai chi, journaling, dancing, creating art, singing or playing music, yoga, most exercise, being outside in nature, inspirational reading, and mindful breathing, to name a few. Explore what works best for you.

Larry is an exemplar of the power of a steady practice. Every day he gets out of bed, puts on his running shoes and clothes, and heads out the door. Living here in the Northwest means a lot of those mornings are wet and cold, a sharp contrast to a warm bed. But 40 minutes later Larry's back, and soon he's showered, dressed, and making breakfast for his wife. He's retired now, so he could sleep in if he wanted to. He's in great shape, and he's the most cheerful guy I know. I asked Larry once how he could maintain such a discipline day after day.

He laughed. "You only know the Larry who starts his day running. If you had known me 10 years ago, you probably wouldn't even be talking to me. I was prone to depression most of my life, and could be a real jerk to the people around me. When my first marriage ended, I bunked with a friend who convinced me to go running with him every day. The short story is, it saved my life."

Larry went on. "See, I don't wake up a nice guy. But I know that if I start every day this way, I'm sweeter, smarter, and sexier! Running does that for me. I've come to love running. It's my time in nature, time to myself, time to remember all that I'm grateful for. Like having the good sense to never give up this practice!"

· · · · · · ·

The goal of life is to make your heartbeat match the beat of the universe, to match your nature with Nature.

Joseph Campbell

· · · · · · ·

PRACTICE
Aligning with the Flow

• • • •

This practice, like all the practices that follow, is based on your capacity to Attend to and Adjust your state: how you Orient and Inhabit yourself. Bring yourself back into the flow and allow restoration, inspiration, and serenity into your daily life. Tune in to your intuition. In his book *Power vs. Force,* David Hawkins refers to intuition as "the capacity to instantaneously understand without resorting to sequential symbol processing." Let it be easy!

At least five minutes a day, or whenever you feel yourself Forcing or fretting or squeezing down:

1. Turn your attention and energy away from your current focus.
2. Watch for any signs of contraction and forcing.
3. Breathe deeply and let your body soften and relax.
4. Intentionally take time for stillness, and open all your receptor sites.
5. Turn your attention to what feeds you, inspires you, widens your sense of possibilities, makes you feel at home in the universe, adds to your resilience.
6. Ask and listen for the answer to these questions:

How easy does this want to be?
What wants to come into form?
What is optimal?
What is it time for?
You may get an answer immediately, or it may come to you later in any number of surprising ways.
7. Stay open and permeable. That means stopping for more than five minutes, overachievers! The more you practice, the easier it becomes to rest here.

. . . .

Take rest. A field that has rested yields a valuable crop.

Ovid

. . . .

Your job is not to figure everything out. Your job is to tune in and become available to infinite possibility. This is about having a hearty appetite with an assurance that you'll be nourished. Trade your tendency to try hard in favor of inspiration. You're giving up separation and choosing a sense of belonging. You're exchanging worry and intensity for fulfillment and delight.

. . . .

When the soul wishes to experience something, she throws an
image of the experience before her and enters into her own image.

Meister Eckhart

. . . .

Attracting: Irresistible Confidence

Think of something about which you are absolutely certain, such as your home address or the color of your car. This is the energy of Attracting. No anxiety. No worry or doubt. Just plain old confidence. You're self-assured and at ease. That relaxed energy—when applied to your intended outcome—is like the lighting on an airport runway. That attitude signals to your heart's desire that it's safe to land . . . right here in your life.

Here's a classic story. A farming community is facing one of the worse droughts in a decade. A few more days and the crops will be ruined, and everyone in town knows that will mean a very lean year for all of them. Someone decides the situation calls for desperate measures, and a town prayer meeting is called at the church. That evening everyone shows up and squeezes into the sanctuary to pray for rain. Only one little girl arrives with an umbrella.

Here's the amazing truth: You don't Attract what you want, or even what you deserve. You Attract what you *expect*. Think of expectation as similar to mood; it's the lens through which you're looking. Your mood colors your predictions about the future, and that is the precise sort of future you begin to expect. You come into relationship with that future long before it appears.

········

Don't question enthusiasm.

Rumi

········

The way in which you focus your energy and attention, and the way you relate to whatever you're focusing on is Attracting. When you're inside the Circle and have a desire for something, you're easefully relating to it as a reality and that simple fact gives it substance. In this way, you begin Attracting it toward you. Conversely, whenever you're outside the Circle longing for something, your desire arises from a sense of separation. It's a way of focusing on your desired outcome that reinforces its distance from you. Yearning and longing, those two hues of hopelessness, actually push away your dreams.

This is where most people get stuck. To get what they want, they try *wanting harder*. They yearn more deeply, try harder to become worthy. They build the case about why they should have what they want, but this very attitude requires holding the desire as other (out of reach). It's a strange paradox that when you want a thing, you affirm that your life is wanting. You affirm the Trance of Scarcity and lack. The Story and Soma of someone who is focused on what is missing is very different from the Story and Soma of someone who confidently expects what he desires. One claims separation as his base camp, while the other relaxes in the warmth of wholeness and belonging.

Monique became a single mother when she was 19 years old. Before that she had lived in foster homes, had been treated despicably on multiple occasions, and lived at the poverty level for over three years. When I met Monique, she was refreshingly honest and insightful, able to tell her life story without bitterness.

"How can you be so generous and positive, given the experiences you've had?" I asked.

She smiled. "My history doesn't define me. I get to do that. And I know that my son and I will have a wonderful life."

In just a few short years, I watched Monique go from working as a waitress to attending an excellent college on scholarship; from being shy to becoming a community spokesperson for child advocacy; from being single to marrying one of the finest men I've ever had the pleasure to know.

Was Monique worthy? Absolutely. Did she want what she got? You bet she did. But what made her irresistible to her desire was her steady confidence. She did not leave the welcome mat out for worry and doubt. She rested in a sense of assurance. In this way, Monique came into relationship with the life she was attracting long before all the details of her life matched up with her vision.

A great finder of bargains, Monique knew how to shop at garage sales and thrift stores. Her wardrobe was campy and innovative; I marveled at the creative way she put things together. After a Saturday excursion to her neighborhood flea market, Monique called with excitement about an old fashioned trunk she had found.

"My future husband will love this! He must be getting close," she chirped.

The trunk was indeed amazing. Sturdy, ornate, and loaded with charm, Monique's find stood nearly four feet tall. She now had a place to put all the things she had lovingly collected over the years for the man she knew she was going to marry.

Monique began taking great pleasure in her anticipation of her husband's arrival. It was like watching someone who's preparing to take a long trip—they get immersed in maps and guidebooks, imaging what they'll be doing. There's no anxiety to stifle their confidence; they start enjoying the journey before they've even packed their bags. It's the opposite of my attitude in high school when I was pining near the phone, praying for that young man to call me. I wasn't confident, so I hovered and fretted and wadded my energy into a knot.

On Monique's wedding day (she met her husband a few months after her flea market find heralded his imminent arrival), she presented the groom with the trunk, now loaded with gifts, and spoke of the way she had been preparing for him to show up. "I knew you were coming," she said, "so I've been collecting things to give you. This is my dowry to you, my belief in us." Remembering her words still gives me shivers.

· · · · · · ·

An abundance mentality springs from internal security,
not from external rankings, comparisons, opinions,
possessions, or associations.

Stephen Covey

· · · · · · ·

Turn Down the Noise, Turn Up the Music

The Kahunas, the wisdom priests of Hawaii, become powerful in the arts of healing and manifestation because they are raised from childhood to live entirely free of doubt. Imagine how it would feel not to have one iota of energy or time siphoned away by worrying and grasping. The Kahunas are immune to the Trance of Scarcity. Their confident knowing leaves no room for doubt or fear to take hold.

A few days ago around three in the morning, I woke up with a sore throat. As a menopausal woman who is too often awake at this hour, I admit this is rarely my best time. It's often when the Trance begins to insist that "it's all downhill from here."

Sure enough, my first thoughts were, "Oh no, it always starts with a sore throat, then it's a full blown cold that lasts a week. Damn! I don't have time for this." I lay there half awake wondering why this had happened and being fearful about how I was going to make up the lost time being sick.

When at last I grudgingly got up to gargle with warm salt water, I looked in the mirror and caught a glimpse of my pitiful face. I had to laugh. I thought, "I may as well *demand* that I'm going to have a cold. I couldn't be attracting it any quicker!" I realized that I was *fully expecting* the arrival of a cold. What we *expect* trumps what we desire every time.

I asked myself, "What would I be thinking and feeling if, despite my symptoms, I fully expected uninterrupted good health and a peaceful night's sleep?" The answer was that I would be relaxed and at ease, looking forward to tomorrow. I would settle into my pillow feeling grateful and happy. Seeing that the option was right there waiting for me, I shifted my state, pronto. I went back to bed excited about how great tomorrow was going to be. The next day I was happily at work at my computer with my favorite Latin-American music blasting in the background—and not the slightest trace of a sore throat.

Attracting   Grasping

Magic? No. It is simply the reliable power of confident expectation. My shortcut version is to affirm that *it already is*. Whatever you want to attract, treat it as if it's already here. You do this in the same way that Monique felt certain she was about to meet the man who would be her husband; in the same way that I affirmed my health in the same way that you know your street address or the color of your car. It doesn't take any more effort than that. In fact, more effort would indicate you are *trying hard to get something*, which, as I mentioned before, actually reveals that you don't accept that *it already is*. Does this attitude require consistent attention? Yes. Effort? No.

Abundance flows freely to us, and yet it's not personal. The flow doesn't treat us as separate. It's not because we've been good girls and boys, or that it's our turn, or because this time we have a really good idea. The universe is biased toward life. Whatever is life-affirming gets universal support.

· · · · · · ·

Concerning all acts of initiative and creation, there is one elementary truth the ignorance of which kills countless ideas and splendid plans: that the moment one definitely commits oneself, then Providence moves too.
All sorts of things occur to help one that would never otherwise have occurred. A whole stream of events issue from the decision, raising in one's favor all manner of unforeseen incidents, meetings and material assistance which no man can have dreamed would have come his way.
Whatever you can do or dream you can, begin it. Boldness has genius, power and magic in it. Begin it now.

W. H. Murray

· · · · · · ·

This statement is often invoked to encourage people to make commitments. I see it, rather, as a testimony to the power of attention and confidence, a reflection of the phenomena that takes place when your assurance makes you so irresistible that the universe wants to conspire on your behalf. In other words, name it and know it!

Look around you. People who are positive are attractive. And they don't seem to work at it, either. They are full of energy and focus. With such wholeheartedness comes a lightheartedness. Positive people seem to glide over the same terrain that makes others slow to a trudge. Are they just lucky? Are they exempt from suffering? No. In fact, the most positive, confident people I know have chosen that *way of being* after experiencing some very hard knocks.

Positive people generate an energy field that others want to join. In that energy, life-affirming creativity and collaboration thrive. By contrast, in the energy of struggle and separation, which require the squeezing down of life force, creativity withers. The British biologist Rupert Sheldrake called this the *morphogenetic field*, the energy field of consciousness, or formative causation.

"Yeah, but what about reality?" the skeptics protest. "Just because you expect something doesn't make it so!" To that, Humberto Maturana (who studied the biology of cognition) would say, "There is no reality independent of the observer." Quantum physics asserts much the same thing. In fact, science continues to build the case for the creative power of Attracting. We're not inventing some tricky way to make things turn out the way we want. We're simply recognizing and making more masterful use of what is already in place.

. . . .

It's a funny thing about life; if you refuse to accept anything but the best, you very often get it.

Somerset Maugham

. . . .

Scan through your own experience for a moment. When you expect things to be hard, they are. When you expect your body to gain weight, it does. Now this is different from what you may want, and that's exactly the point. Again, you don't Attract what you want; you Attract what you expect. Expectation is a magnet because it's undiluted energy. And Attracting is simply a matter of matching energy for energy.

Most of us have put in overtime focusing on what we want, not getting it, and then finding some explanation for why we didn't get it: I didn't deserve it. God didn't want me to have it. This stuff doesn't work. I'm just unlucky. Life is unfair. But as it turns out, all of those are just Stories and superstitions. They're not Truth. That story-line is the very essence of Grasping. It insists that we can *make* bad things happen by following the wrong formula.

Like Murray and Maturana, scientists who mastered the art of observation, we need to recognize the formula that *does* work. That formula is not desire but confident expectation. It's an example of energy matching energy, impersonal but reliable. When you pray for rain, bring an umbrella.

When Everything Is Possible, Nothing Is Necessary

Most people never experience a higher standard of living than their parents enjoyed. They're conditioned to expect a certain quality of life, and they get busy proving those parameters. Consider the very wealthy, for example. It doesn't occur to them *not* to be wealthy. They expect money to flow, they expect their needs to be met, they expect to live in the world with ease. And they do. Even if they lose great sums of money, they quickly amass it again.

Growing up just above middle class in the 1950s (my dad was a career military officer), I knew what to expect. I would go to college using my parents' savings, get a decent job, work for a living, earn my way up. If I worked all the details just right, I could manage a home about as nice as my parents had been able to buy. That would be *success*, and that was within my range of possibility.

Fast forward to the 90s. Driving to the airport, my friend Jim and I were discussing our future hopes and ambitions, as we often did. Almost in passing, he said, "Oh, Victoria, money is never going to be an issue for you." It's a good thing he was driving. Suddenly the landscape disappeared, and if he said something more I didn't hear it. His words ricocheted inside my body and brain. They felt really good and I wanted them to stay. Could I somehow sew them into my lining permanently?

I trusted Jim. I saw him as a mentor, so what he said carried extra weight with me. But I also knew that it wasn't Jim who needed to believe those words. In that moment, I knew I could make a life-changing decision. I chose to accept his statement as my reality. It wasn't because I gave Jim's words authority; it was because I gave *my* words authority.

I decided there and then that I would never worry about money again. My Soma softened and began embodying an upgraded Story. The future looked so bright, I had to wear shades.

. . . .

Fear is the expectation of pain, so its opposite is the expectation of pleasure. The world is what you think it is.

Serge Kahili King

. . . .

Certainly I've had opportunities to test my expectations. And when I fell into the potholes laid in my path by the Trance of Scarcity, I recognized them for what they were—variations of a useless Story—and climbed out as quickly as I could. But here's where the power really resided: I knew my wholeness was not at risk. Whether I had money or not had nothing to do with my worth, or my belonging in the Circle. Whether I was scraping pennies together or enjoying a windfall, my circumstances were simply showing me the shape of my own expectations.

My divorce, my father's death, my year of unemployment and hand-to-mouth living had proven to me that whatever life delivered, I could deal with it. *Go ahead, Life, give me your best shot,* I thought. *I am whole regardless of circumstance.* It was an attitude that granted true freedom. At last I realized that my experience of Abundance was determined by my inner state rather than by my outer circumstances, and as far as my inner state was concerned, I had complete dominion.

Interestingly, this new awareness softened the edges of expectation. Now I expect a steady flow of money, but I'm not monitoring how it happens. It's not something I think about constantly, working out every detail. In fact, I treat the details as though they're *none of my business.* Why limit infinite possibility? In contrast, the state of Grasping is fascinated with details because it thinks it has to manage them all.

So if you want money, expect money. Don't limit the ways in which money can come to you by thinking too specifically about it. Your Abundance might come through your work, or it might come through some fluke, like a surprise refund for a set of tires you bought three years ago. That happened to me once. The refund check for the tires arrived on the same day a certain bill was due, and the amounts matched almost to the penny! Now when I do turn my thoughts to money, it's with a great sense of gratitude. You can decide to allow Abundance to come to you in whatever way it likes. You're whole, regardless. Be at ease.

. . . .

*The power that lies behind manifestation arises from a state of
wholeness. It is the vision and experience of this wholeness that we
wish to cultivate, for it is the source of power for our
acts of manifestation.*

David Spangler

. . . .

Now here comes the curveball. I encourage you to confidently expect, while not being attached to an outcome. Expect it, but then let it go. Yes, the money would be great, the job would be perfect, the relationship would be wonderful, but they in themselves are not what has value. It's what they *provide* that we are really interested in—the sense of security or freedom, the experience of happiness and belonging. We can claim those states as our inner reality, with or without the associated tangibles. It's the essence behind the form that really matters to us. And when we live in It Already Is, we are irresistible to the flow of Abundance in the universe.

PRACTICE
Attracting with Confidence
• • • •

Begin to get chummy with Abundance; get used to hanging out with it, let it be part of your daily life. Pick one area: money, relationships, work, home, health. Practice focusing on it with confidence until you feel a firm sense of positive expectation in that area. Then move on to your next area of focus. Here are the steps in the process.

1. Be clear about what you want and why. Identify the essence behind the form.

2. Feel as if It Already Is. Make it vivid. Take time to breathe it in, taste it, see from its viewpoint. Fully live the experience. Don't settle for a vague image or memory.

3. Merge with it. It's already here; you can't be separated from it.

4. Get into that Soma and speak that Story. Stay here until you

are satisfied that there is no Grasping going on within you.

5. Savor this reality, full of gratitude and assurance.

6. Hold this state confidently and lightly, without attach-ment. Enjoy being already whole.

7. When you slip into worrying or Grasping, hop out as quickly as you can without fear or recrimination. Then repeat the above steps until you feel at ease again.

Hint: Confidence is cumulative. The more time and focus you direct in the practice of confidence, the more potent it becomes.

The universe doesn't consider you separate, so you don't need to convince anyone but yourself that you can have what you want. Living in confident expectation means using your energy most effi-ciently; it's the way to live life by design rather than by default. Direct your energy! Remember, it doesn't matter how much you want something. Wanting is self-perpetuating—if that's where your energy is focused, you'll just get more wanting.

Time for a pop quiz. Your role in relation to Abundance is

(a) Making the right phone call at just the right time.

(b) Pleading your case to an unresponsive universe.

(c) Being really, really good.

(d) Creating a backup plan, just in case.

(e) Knowing IT ALREADY IS.

If you chose (a) through (d) it's time to take the garbage out, because the Trance virus is alive and it will spread fast in all that rotting compost. If you chose (e), you've prob-ably stopped reading and are over at a friend's house savor-ing what is. *Bon appétit!*

8
Chapter

Receiving and Gratitude

O ur dog Ginger dedicated her life to pleasure, ours as well as hers. She taught us to walk in the woods, but always seemed a little disappointed that we never learned to get down and sniff and roll and pounce. Ginger would race ahead on the trail, then stop and turn, puzzled that we weren't barreling after her, following suit. Didn't we want to have fun, romp, and be happy? Endlessly patient, Ginger never gave up on our education. Many of her lessons unfolded in our own backyard.

When you live in the Pacific Northwest, as we do, every moment of sunshine is precious. Ginger's personal research project was discovering how much sun and heat one dog could absorb on any given day. In the morning she started on the red brick patio near the back door so she could face and welcome the eastern rays. When the sunlight was eventually blocked by the cedar trees, Ginger would move from her established warm spot to the far edge of the patio, reassume her position, and *absorb*. Wherever the sun went, Ginger followed. By afternoon she had relocated her sun spa to the lawn, and after a few more hours of proper baking, she repaired to the flower bed, once again settling in to soak up the warm sunlight. By late afternoon, the shadow of the house intruded upon this tactic and a new strategy was called for.

When the angle of the sun could no longer make direct contact with the ground, Ginger would raise her head to catch its long rays. I often watched her literally leaning into the light, lifting her chin and closing her eyes in those last moments of communion. On Ginger's watch, the sun could retire each day satisfied that not one ray of warmth had gone to waste.

Not a moment of Ginger's day was wasted, either. Whatever presented itself, she took part in it with enthusiasm. Going for a walk, riding in the car, greeting guests, eating, chasing a ball, rolling in something putrid, seeking out the warmth of the sun—to every moment, Ginger made herself completely available. I envied how confident she was about the way she showed up. It spoke to me of a heart that lived wide open.

From Ginger I learned the key to receiving: being permeable, accessible, available. This might sound a little risky to you, and if it does, rest assured you're not alone. There's a lot of stuff out there I don't necessary want to feel, either. This is particularly true if I'm not used to feeling much and have intentionally dialed down the volume on life to keep it and myself under control. Ah, the illusion of *control*. The word comes from the French *contra rolare*, referring to the wedge that was placed under the wheel of a cart to keep it from rolling forward (and hence, spinning out of control). As much as we might like to keep things still and quiet, trying to get life to stay put is a fruitless strategy. Margaret Wheatley writes that the essential issue we face in life is not being in control, but being connected. If we develop the capacity to meet whatever life serves up, to truly connect with it, we uncover a mysterious secret—the power to let life expand and enrich us.

． ． ． ． ． ． ．

To receive, we must be alert, awake, and prepared to receive.

Matthew Fox

． ． ． ． ． ． ．

Receiving: Being Satisfiable

In the Cycle of Abundance, Receiving is the depth of the inhale. It's a big "Yes, thank you, I accept." Through a strictly puritanical lens, Receiving looks selfish and indulgent. Here, though, we're committed to a different kind of seeing. Receiving means consenting to be a conduit for the flow of all life to move through us, as we take our place in the Circle. Those of us who want to do good in the world are especially accountable to our own well-being. If we are to be of real service to humanity, we must make ourselves available to be nourished, inspired, and sustained. Otherwise, how would we keep going? Burnout is an all too common experience.

When we don't believe there will be enough, or when we're afraid the good things in life won't last—it's then that we overindulge. In eating, for example, if we've been depriving or restricting ourselves, as soon as the forbidden food comes within reach we must have it *now* (and usually all of it). This happens when we're out of touch with our actual appetite, with the awareness about which foods would be nourishing and satisfying. When we deprive ourselves, it only creates more urgency to fill a hole, the hole of deprivation!

Overindulging or acting unconsciously is quite different from being lavish. When we are lavish, we inhabit the unconflicted realm of *Yes*—wholehearted and intentional enthusiasm for life, in the same way that Ginger continually reoriented herself to welcome the gift of sunshine. When we make strict rules for ourselves about what is allowed and how we may feel, we're being stingy with ourselves. That stinginess leads to frustration, suspicion, righteous anger, and, ultimately, grim resignation. If we don't believe we can have what we want, we unconsciously create lifestyles that assure we can't possibly be fulfilled.

Receiving   *Numbing*

Much of our time-honored cultural and religious training tells us that having plenty will make us spiritually shallow. But such an approach only perpetuates struggle as our standard *way of being*. I don't know about you, but not being able to pay my rent has never done much to deepen my spiritual understanding! Whether our goal is fulfillment through the world of sensual delights or through the depth of spiritual insight, our first task is the same: We must get in touch with what truly satisfies us.

The degree of our joy isn't a matter of how much (money or time or stuff or privilege or fame or love or freedom) we have. It's about *how we are* with what we have. What is your relationship with everything you have in your life? We all know of people whose obsession with getting more makes them miserable. We may also know of people with plenty of money who are not attached to their possessions, who live comfortably but simply, and who are deeply spiritual. Some folks possessed of very little material wealth nevertheless embody a calm, detached simplicity. Rich or poor, we all have the option to worry and fret and obsess in an effort to hold on to whatever we have.

There's no official chart that we can check to make sure that we have enough, that we've arrived at the right amount. Once again, it's not about *how much*; it's about whether we attempt to control the flow or *simply trust it*. Have you ever tried to hold a beach ball under water? With much of your energy and attention absorbed in keeping a bobbing inflatable submerged and under control, are you really enjoying the water? You may be surrounded by pleasure, but only if you're aware—if you're fully available to the experience of the water, for example—can you enjoy it.

Moving naturally with the flow of life always comes down to this: your state. What is your inner experience, your lived experience in the body, when you're holding on? (Hint: think of the term *tightwad*.) When you Inhabit and Orient yourself as being in the flow—when you really settle in and begin to embody it—a wonderful thing happens: you acquire the spontaneous ability to *sense* what is best for you. The Trance of Scarcity, on the other hand, will always point you toward dissatisfaction. If you listen to the Trance, you can absolutely count on seeing what you don't have. Seeing lack, you'll start straining for more. That ever-elusive *more*—did you ever notice how *more* is an unattainable amount? *More* is a trap!

When we seek *more* we join the long line of the chronically empty, knocking again and again at the wrong address, hoping for fulfillment. We fill our plates at the all-you-can-eat buffet and then have to stop at the drugstore on our way home to load up on antacids. When we've worked hard all day, we reward ourselves by picking up the remote control and waiting to be entertained, then climb into bed with a vague sense of discomfort and discontent. We've all done these things, knowing they were only temporary relief for a deeper ailment. When we finally reach the heart of the matter, however, we instantly understand that the flow is constant and inexhaustible. Realizing that we are part of the flow, we are freed from the burden of accumulation.

· · · · · · ·

Not what we have, but what we enjoy,
constitutes our abundance.

John Petit-Senn

· · · · · · ·

Years ago I spent three glorious autumn days in Yosemite National Park. Everywhere I looked, I was confronted with inspiring beauty: Majestic cliffs were poised like heroes above the meandering rivers and fields. Fluffy clouds paraded overhead, and the changing leaves drifted across the scene like a painting in constant motion. Intoxicating!

On the morning of our departure, while my companions packed their bags, I walked into the field near our cabin. One last time, I wanted to take in this luscious experience of nature at her best. I took a deep breath to allow myself to be filled with it. That wasn't big enough, so I took in the next breath even more deeply and intentionally. I was determined to take the experience with me, so I became even more intentional. Soon my entire focus was on breathing in all this beauty, in just the right way. A few more breaths and I felt downright inadequate!

All that work to become more conscious, spiritual, and enlightened, I thought, *and I can't have an experience of union, even when I'm surrounded by natural splendor!* I replanted my feet, determined to get this right. Maybe I was just too small a container.

Okay, I pouted to my uncooperative surroundings, *I can't seem to grow large enough to absorb you, so . . . au revoir.* I turned to go inside, feeling dejected and a little ripped off. But suddenly I heard something rumbling deep inside me. I stopped in my tracks to listen. "How about if you let *us* absorb *you?*" it was saying. Dumbstruck, I turned back toward the mountains, and all my armor of disappointment and unworthiness dissolved in an instant. My heart swelled with delight. As though I had just seen a long-absent friend, I opened my arms and giggled like a child. We merged, those majestic mountains, those verdant meadows and trees, that big sky, and I. I let the whole scene absorb me and . . . *ta da!* At last I knew the oneness I had longed for.

I often revisit that day and that pivotal moment. A wise person once said that if you go to the ocean with a tiny cup, you'll only take away a little water. I had mistakenly thought that the reason I felt cut off from the beauty around me was because I hadn't presented a large enough container. But in fact, it was because I insisted on having any container at all! When at last I dropped all boundaries and limits on what was flowing toward me, simply letting the scene wash over and through me, it made all the difference. By engaging the soft power of Receiving, I was able to be expanded and enriched by that moment. It was a gift of deep satisfaction that went far beyond the outer beauty I was witnessing. That experience has changed me. Now I can allow myself to be affected by life in all its beauty, wonder, kindness, and sorrow. **I can receive more because I can feel more.**

· · · · · · ·

Life is in the breath. He who half-breathes, half-lives.

Chinese Proverb

· · · · · · ·

Common Acts as Voluptuous Experiences

The more we can feel (the more aliveness we can allow in our system), the more present we can be to ourselves, to others, and to the experiences of life. Aliveness is the sense of really being present: sensory awareness, emotional awareness, conscious awareness. The more aliveness we can handle, the more we are available to the flow of life within us.

Ginger's basking in the sun and my epiphany at Yosemite National Park are examples of being fully available to the moment. That's where magic happens. Brian Swimme, a mathematical cosmologist and author of *The Universe Is a Green Dragon*, talks about the ability to be enchanted, the capacity to be touched and to become absorbed. To all of you who would like more excitement, pleasure, and satisfaction in your lives, please take note: Enchantment is self-serve. Opportunities abound, *if you are available.*

I've had the pleasure of officiating at more than a hundred weddings in the last decade. For me, the experience is pure pleasure; I am usually the most relaxed person in attendance. For the bride and groom and other members of the wedding party, the event can be stressful to the point of counting the minutes until it's over. They can tend to go a little bit, shall we say, Numb.

Of the many celebrations that mark people's lives, a couple's wedding is one event during which they most want to be present and fully alive. They want to feel their love and commitment to each other. But unless they have previously developed a capacity for aliveness, their system (their psychobiology) will tend to squeeze down in such life-altering situations. We have all learned too well how to shorten our breath, tighten our muscles, close off, and shut down until we can get through whatever seems to be too much for us.

As you might guess, whenever I see the almost-newlyweds begin to glaze over, I intervene. We talk about it, laugh about it a little; I encourage them to take a few deep breaths, drink a little water, walk around a bit, look at the sky, and remember what this big event in their lives called a *wedding* is all about: the two of them and their love for each other. In the weeks before the ceremony, I have given them a few Somatic practices to help them prepare for all the love that will be focused on them on their wedding day. There's a good reason for the term *receiving line*. That's exactly what it is. The bride and groom receive the loving support and enthusiasm of their line—their friends and extended family—in a direct, sustained, and immediate way, up close.

Squeezin' Ain't Always Pleasin'

The opposite of Receiving is Numbing. When we go Numb, we avoid letting ourselves be touched or expanded by our life experience. Instead, we vacate the premises. We do this by closing all sensory entry points so that we feel as little as possible. Sadly, this is a pattern most of us perfected, if not in early childhood, then as teenagers when being cool became more important than just about anything else. To *be cool* usually means to show no reaction. To do this convincingly, of course, requires *having* no reaction—which, in turn, requires separating yourself from your feelings. Failing that, we may have developed an amazing capacity to fake it. Either way, our life force has had to operate in a tiny alley out back.

· · · · · · ·

The biggest human temptation is to settle for too little.

Thomas Merton

· · · · · · ·

You can deepen your capacity for aliveness by practicing how you receive the *good* things that come to you. Right now, look around and find three things that please you, and just let yourself feel and appreciate them about 10 percent more. What you choose might be as simple as the comfortable temperature of the room, the color of your shirt, or the view from a window. When students in my Somatics classes try this exercise, they're always surprised at how much different and better they suddenly feel.

Few of us have been taught to open up to the enjoyment of life. Instead, we're taught to squeeze tight. But the sad truth is that keeping ourselves and our feelings under control instantly shuts off our capacity for pleasure. In fact, we may need to practice the opposite behavior at times. My very classy friend, Betty, taught me years ago that too much decorum can get in the way of enjoyment. Sometimes, she said, you just need to lick the plate, even in a four-star restaurant!

When you keep yourself set on low, or Numb, you have to go on the hunt for something to make you feel alive. You become dependent on something outside of you to affect you enough and in just the right way. This is pretty much the description of the victim mentality: Something out there is responsible for my happiness. Seeking something outside yourself to provide satisfaction is a recipe for addiction and consumerism, and ultimately a life unfulfilled. Eve Ensler, the cutting-edge playwright of *The Vagina Monologues* and *The Good Body*, says that capitalism pushed to its extreme becomes "a malignant or atrophied narcissism where you become so self-focused that you are just a commodity that needs to consume to exist." Numbness keeps us unfulfilled.

As we have seen, it isn't certain *things* that satisfy us, it is our capacity to be satisfied. Are you satisfiable? Notice that I'm not saying you should settle for less; rather, I'm suggesting that you develop the capacity to Receive more. The last line of Derek Walcott's poem "Love After Love" says it beautifully: "Sit. Feast on your life." What are you presented with that you might fully Receive in this moment, this place, this income, this age, this you, this life? Whatever it is: Sit. Feast.

·······

*There are two ways to live life: One as if nothing is a miracle,
the other as if everything is.*

Albert Einstein

·······

PRACTICE
Receiving

• • • •

Take out your magic wand now, and enchant yourself by turning the ordinary into the voluptuous. Note as you do that *voluptuous* simply means *the unrestricted pleasure of the senses*, so you'll want every one of your senses participating fully in this practice.

1) Begin with your state. Inhabit and Orient yourself so that you are fully present and as open as possible. Scan for the most subtle contraction and then let it go. Or, if you like, begin by intentionally tightening up and squeezing yourself down. Then . . . let go and scan for any residual holding. Let that go, too. Keep a soft and open belly, relaxed muscles and joints, free, easy breathing. Focus your attention on taking in more of what is being offered to you right now, in this very moment.

2) Find at least three occasions every day to engage in deep pleasure and real satisfaction. Try focusing on routine actions: driving your car, typing at the computer, brushing your teeth, grocery shopping, waiting in line, drink-

ing water, answering the phone, walking to a meeting, watering houseplants, even taking out the trash.

3) Whenever you feel bored, impatient, burdened, or Numb, try amping up your Receiving volume. Ask yourself, "If I were more available right now, in this moment, what new possibilities might that create?"

4) Watch for how this practice impacts your energy, creativity, and interactions with others. Make a habit of being enriched by the moments of your life.

. . . .

Life itself is the proper binge!

Julia Child

. . . .

The very best gift you can Receive is yourself, really fully to embrace and receive *you*. I learned an important lesson about this from my father, a hard-working, hard-driving man. He came from deep poverty and worked his way through college to a successful and decorated career in the military. To my knowledge, he was never satisfied. And you bet he pushed his kids. His message, drilled into us from an early age, was *You've got to be the best or you have no business taking up space!* Underneath that command was the demand for perfection. *Get in there. Work harder. You can do better. Don't be a loser.* It took me years to realize that all his life, my father had been bullying *himself* with the same relentless insistence.

Decades later, having worked hard on a daily basis to prove my worth, I had grown weary of my career of self-improvement. That was when I received a message from my dad. It was so out of character that at first I couldn't believe it had come from him. It turned out to be his final and most precious gift to me.

"You know all that stuff I told you about how you had to be good enough, how you had to be the best?" he said. "Remember how I told you that you had to work hard and never be satisfied, that there was always room for improvement, and everything? Well, forget it! It doesn't matter. In the end, all that matters is giving and receiving love. And receiving is more important than giving."

I was stunned. While I could grasp the part about love being what really mattered, I didn't know what to make of his having said that receiving was more important than giving. I respected my father's new attitude, but how could it be true? It is more blessed to give than to receive—that was the biblical advice I had grown up with, and I was still deeply interested in earning "blessed" status. I had gotten very good at pretending not to have any needs. Now I was supposed to just give all that up?

Over the next few months I pondered why Receiving was so important. It was a tough assignment for an overachiever, but I knew my dad was on to something. By then I was coaching executives for a living. With alarming consistency, I encountered people for whom burnout and over commitment had been their downfall. Gradually I began to understand: If your tank is empty, you can't fill up anyone else. I began to imagine what might be different in my life if I really started Receiving, accepting my share, and I saw how different that would feel. Doing this, I also realized how much of my giving I did when my own tank was sitting on Empty—how I was using giving to others in a doomed attempt to fill myself up.

This is why the Cycle of Abundance is a cycle, not a straight line. If the flow is allowed to follow its natural course, it always replenishes itself. The inhale allows the exhale to follow. Being able to Receive—to let yourself be filled and replenished, expanded and opened up—frees you to flow with the best of them. Then your giving becomes more authentic, more enlivening and satisfying. You're present for the whole ride.

Gratitude: Deepening Your Connection

Gratitude focuses your attention. For this reason, it affects what you see and how you move. Energy follows attention. This law proves itself over and over, and it applies to the practice of Gratitude as well. Right now, listen to the sounds around you. Now focus on your breath. Now think of a task you need to complete. Do you notice that whatever you focus on becomes more real to you? Richard Strozzi-Heckler writes, "When we're not paying attention, we miss life. When we're awake and alive, we are participants in life. What we pay attention to becomes a world in which we can participate. And what we pay attention to becomes our reality."

There it is: Reality. How we Inhabit and Orient our lives determines what constitutes reality for each of us. People who operate in a state of Gratitude are consistently more creative, joyful, connected, resilient, and peaceful than those who operate inside the Trance of Scarcity, which perpetuates criticism and complaint. I know; I've done thorough personal research in both camps.

Victoria's Adventures in Hell

As mentioned earlier, it was not my favorite year. My 11-year "perfect marriage" ended, my father died, I had surgery for a serious health challenge, I left my two beloved dogs behind with my ex, I moved to a new city where I didn't know anyone, I looked for work for six months unsuccessfully, and I was running out of money fast.

Each morning I woke up, realized I was still here, and was crushed at the burden of getting through another day. I'd start the day with prayer and meditation, but this always ended up as whimpering and hollering. I felt lonely and bereft, living inside a perpetual ache. Even chocolate didn't taste good!

I found a church where you weren't thrown out for crying, so I went to worship services, classes, volunteer meetings, any event where other people could be found. One evening I attended a class for the Singles Group at the church. I sat down with my tissues at the ready and beseeched the fates to grant that no one would ask me how I was.

The speaker suggested we write down ten things we were grateful for, every day. Clearly he had not seen *my* life, or he would have been embarrassed to have made such an absurd suggestion. Just exactly what was it that I was supposed to be grateful for? That my husband was hundreds of miles away and therefore I didn't have to run into his pert little girlfriend? That I was overqualified for every job I applied for? That the only extravagance I could indulge in was gasoline for my car?

Later, at home, I figured I'd take a few minutes to prove the guy wrong: there definitely weren't 10 things to be grateful for in my life. I got pen and paper, and numbered one through 10. And waited. Okay, I was grateful for Kleenex because I sure did a lot of crying; that's one. Oh, and long distance phone calls, because talking to my friends and my mom were the only things keeping me sane; that's two. I sat there scanning my everyday life for anything that might make it to the page. *Magnum P.I.* reruns; that was number three. My one daily hour of solace occurred from 5 to 6 PM, Monday through Friday. For that hour I was away at the beach with Magnum, blissfully shielded from my icky, woeful life.

The next day, I again numbered my paper one through 10, still determined to prove this practice was a farce. This time I made it to seven. *Wait, that can't be right!* I whined. *There can't possibly be seven things to be grateful for in my world!* But the truth was, I had furniture,

I had electricity, I had windows to press my forehead against and sigh. Oh, and there was also color and light, and eyes to see them with, and a car that always started. That was seven, and while I was sure I deserved infinitely more, I was pretty glad about those seven.

Though I expected the lack of anything good in my life to continue indefinitely, nice things kept insinuating themselves into my awareness. Blessings began showing up everywhere. I continued doing the gratitude practice, and I kept finding more things to add to my list. Sunglasses, keys that worked, chewing gum, stoplights, toilet paper, running water, fingernail files, mail, toothpaste, matches, hot tea, clean sheets, Cary Grant movies, drinking straws, being literate, trash bags, shade trees, salt, safe walking trails, fresh tomatoes, paved roads, good writing pens, music, the public library, birds singing, the ongoing kindness of strangers. Hey!

The steel door to my cage had opened only a crack, but that was enough. Gradually I began to experience moments of actual happiness. They were tiny moments, but they were real. If this was the result of being grateful, it was well worth it! Soon I made it all the way to 10 things on my list, day after day. Pretty soon I couldn't stop at 10 because the more I looked, the more blessings I saw, and the happier I became. For awhile I remained watchful for the other shoe to drop. *Okay, it feels good right now, but I know it can't last.* But I can now report that, nearly two decades later, there has been no sign of that other shoe.

. . . .

To speak gratitude is courteous and pleasant, to enact gratitude is generous and noble, but to live gratitude is to touch heaven.

Johannes A. Gastner

. . . .

This was the big surprise: I didn't have to wait for my life to get better in order to feel a level of Gratitude that would lead to the experience of greater joy and peace. As far as feeling Gratitude was concerned, I was a VIP at a ritzy restaurant: I could go right in, sit right down, and survey an endless menu of blessings anytime I liked. Living in Gratitude sweetened the life I was in, just as it was. Not only that, but I also experienced an unexpected release from the grip of fear. I saw how much time I spent dreading the future, wondering what would happen next to make my life even more difficult and vapid. Before the practice of the gratitude list came along, I was clenched and contracted, braced for the worst.

According to Martin Seligman and his work in Learned Optimism, such bracing matches the predisposition of a pessimist. There is a certain tone to the Story of the pessimist, and it stands in sharp contrast to the tone of the optimist's Story. When things don't go well, a pessimist sees the event as permanent and pervasive. When things go well, the pessimist views the event as temporary and specific. In the optimist's view, just the reverse is true. Difficult occurrences are considered temporary and specific, while positive events are treated as permanent and pervasive. In both cases, the Story is the lens that determines the person's view of her life and whether she experiences it as bad or good.

·······

Whenever you are sincerely pleased, you are nourished.

Emerson

·······

Gratitude is generative energy. Gratitude is the art of turning anything into a blessing. It is a view that alters our set point for what is normal, what we expect, what we are open to receiving in life. Gratitude magically expands our capacity for "Yes, thank you."

Increasing Your Tolerance for Bliss

Deepen your appreciation about anything, and watch its value immediately increase. That's the basis of value in real estate, antiques, and great thinkers: all are valuable because they are appreciated. The Institute of Heartmath has done substantial research that shows that *spending just five minutes a day in appreciation* lowers blood pressure and cortisol (the stress hormone), boosts the immune system, and elevates serotonin levels for up to 10 hours. It feels good while you're doing it, and it can make you healthier. That's a double blessing.

If we are not practiced in saying yes to life, then we can forget about bliss—we just want relief! Relief from our hectic lives, from our negative self-talk, from our perpetual fatigue. I used to think that I just had the thermostat set too low, at Relief, and that with a little more practice, I would easily move on up to Bliss. Instead, it turns out that the road to bliss and the road to relief head in completely different directions.

Relief isn't much; it's only an interruption of discomfort. It leads to a nice rest stop with a turnaround that plops you right back on the same road. Bliss, however, is the superhighway to the juiciness if life. As my musician friends Bev Daugherty and Garnett Hundley sing, "Live flat out, eat it all up with a spoon!" Having a high bliss tolerance means you're willing to be pleased by life. And the better it gets, the more you can stand. In this scenario, you anticipate benevolence and are expanded by your experience. When you are consistently grateful, it's impossible to feel like a victim; you know that no matter how well it may be disguised, you can find the blessing in whatever's going on.

The Great Thaw

If you want to dominate people and keep them in fear, teach them to see only what's missing and what's not possible. Program them to believe in scarcity as the only reality. Keep them hoping for little and expecting even less. Soon they will become disheartened and docile, or remote and disengaged. Either way, such folks can be managed easily. When we see this happening in an organization or in a nation, we become outraged. Yet we do the same thing to ourselves every day. We convince ourselves how life is and that things can't work out, and we ridicule any remaining sense of hope we may feel. Arrogance is the opposite of Gratitude.

Doug, a bright young man in his 20s, peered at the world through the peephole of Arrogance, scorning the notion of Gratitude. He saw the world as tiresome and disappointing. Yet he had many reasons to be grateful. He was well educated, extremely intelligent, competent in a field that continues to impact the global economy; he made an excellent living, was in good physical health, lived in a beautiful home, drove a new car, had traveled throughout Europe, and owned many of the latest technological conveniences.

If you had met Doug on the street, though, you would have seen a man with his chest collapsed inward, his head pulled down, muscles tightened around his mouth, dull eyes, arms limp at his sides, legs tense, and breath held in his upper chest.

Stop reading for just a moment now, and take on Doug's Soma; stand up and walk around in it. Notice what happens to your mood, your view of life, your view of yourself.

Living in the Story and Soma of Arrogance kept Douglas wary and critical, distanced from life and from himself. Gratitude, with all its wholeheartedness and expansion, felt like the other side of the universe to him. When I started working with him, I remembered how my own experience of finding Gratitude when I least expected it had taught me the surprising truth that circumstances don't matter, and I knew it would work for Doug, too. We just needed to find an opening. Finally, it was loneliness that moved Doug off his righteous post. He was tired of feeling cut off and separate.

First he learned how to breathe fully, and agreed to practice that. I knew he would do it perfectly; he wouldn't stand for anything less. Then we tried the practice of allowing more aliveness, more feeling, to move throughout his system. This was a tough one for Doug; he was used to clenching down to keep a feeling of control. Since he was a runner, I asked him to simply try becoming more aware of the sensation in his legs while he ran, and to report back about the colors he saw on his run. At first Doug's descriptions were that his legs felt tight, the ground was uneven, and the colors looked "the way they always are this time of year." But as I pushed for details, he kept at it. Soon he had more aliveness in his step, more light in his eyes, and a look on his face of growing curiosity.

When he first started the gratitude list, I told Doug he could write down only things he could see or touch nearby. As Doug began noticing more to be grateful for, he was also connecting more with his surroundings. Before he had plodded numbly through his days, but now he was beginning to notice when another driver made room for him in traffic or how quickly a service rep returned his call. Within a couple of months, he was no longer the sour, dour, dutiful embodiment of Arrogance. He began to reveal a sense of humor, even about himself. Then one day when I needed help with a computer glitch, Doug couldn't have been more gentle and supportive as he talked me through the solution. His natural care and concern for others had begun to seep through.

Arrogance   *Gratitude*

When he says *thank you*, now, Doug really means it. He says he doesn't feel as lonely; he's looking around for a potential girlfriend now that the whole female population looks less silly, troublesome, and needy. This young man had been frozen in Arrogance (trademark of the Trance of Scarcity), and it was a joy to see him come back to life.

It's no small thing to choose to move toward life. Doug relinquished the artificial safety of Arrogance and traded it in for the risky business of being deeply touched and expanded. This is the reality that philosophers ponder and poets muse about. Ships are safe as long as they stay in the harbor, but is that what ships are for?

In any given moment, we make a profound choice—will we move toward life, or move away? If the only response we know is to move away, we can reassure ourselves that we have avoided some of life's hassles. But we will be left wondering why we have missed out on care and love and elation.

Instant Community

Timing is everything. In 1989 my partner Tim and I somehow managed to be within five miles of the epicenter of the Loma Prieta earthquake near San Francisco. The ground shook so hard that our car jumped on the pavement. Chimneys crumbled off houses, palm trees whipped the ground on either side of us, bridges cracked, power lines jerked like lightning bolts, and rush hour traffic came to a halt. We were in Santa Cruz, a lovely seaside town, usually ideal for tourists.

We drove slowly and carefully to a motel a few blocks away, with no high buildings or trees anywhere near. As we entered the lobby, a young and extremely nervous desk clerk was attempting to answer people's questions. Phone lines were down, the power was out. It was just after five o'clock; by seven the town would be completely dark. People were understandably anxious, and yet everyone was checking to make sure that others, strangers, were okay.

We made a joke about the motel's earthquake rates, and suddenly found ourselves part of a community. That night several of us who knew each other only by first names walked in the dark to a small convenience store a few blocks away to buy a little food. Warm 7-Up and a bag of chips had never tasted so good!

The motel was surprisingly full. Among us were a few out-of-state travelers, some people who worked in town and couldn't get home, and several others who had been forced to leave their homes for safer shelter. One man had chain-sawed his way through a series of fallen trees to get down his driveway and into town. A couple with a small child, visiting from the Midwest, had been picnicking at the beach and, concerned about the possibility of a tsunami, kept asking if we were on high enough ground.

The two announcers on the only local radio station authorized as an Emergency Network talked to us all through the night. As tired and scared as they may have been, they stayed at their post for over 12 hours. This was during the time before cell phones, so these guys were our only link to the outside world.

Now, if you've never experienced an earthquake, you may not know about the aftershocks. For the next 48 hours you can expect smaller repetitions of earth-jarring rumblings. That night in the motel, we counted six of them.

All of us lay there in our dark rooms fully clothed, with our doors open to ensure we wouldn't get trapped if we needed to make a fast exit. Tim and I lay on the bed, portable radio on the nightstand, holding hands and talking quietly. When the aftershocks came, we would time them. Twice we each had one foot on the floor ready to bolt. Then the movement would stop, and we'd exhale with relief.

Following each aftershock, we would all call out to check on each other.

"Everyone okay? Anyone need anything?"

"That one lasted a long time, didn't it?"

"Hey, only three more hours before daylight!"

Being so close to disaster that night and during the next few days, I was struck by the apparent fact that what most people wanted was to connect with and reassure others. Complete strangers were drawn to care about each other. When dawn came we were all up, talking, walking around, and basically exchanging kindness. Our mutuality, our belonging, was conspicuous and welcome.

The 20th-century Jewish philosopher Martin Buber wrote about what he called our "essential reciprocity." We do not exist without each other. It is our connectedness, our fundamental belonging that best defines our species. In the time after the earthquake it wasn't every man for himself, it was individuals coming together to help and share and create. Abundance is relational.

PRACTICE
Gratitude

• • • •

Get out pen and paper and start your list. Right away you already have four items to include: paper, pen, the ability to write, and the eyesight that makes it possible to see the page. See how quickly you can get to 10.

1) Check in with yourself. Why bother to be grateful? What difference does it make?

2) Without changing anything, scan your state and rate how expanded you are, with Arrogant being on the low end and Grateful on the high end. Could you expand 2 percent more? 10 percent more? What would that make possible?

3) By all means, list at least 10 things you are grateful for, and do it every day. But do more than write them down: experience them. Five minutes of appreciation boosts your immune system for the whole day.

4) Notice who you feel grateful to and why. Have you told them? Feel your connection to them. Enjoy your essential reciprocity.

5) Now start blessing everything you see, everything you think about. Bless even the things that are a little harder to feel grateful for, at first glance.

In the scarcity model, being grateful requires us to acknowledge that we are unworthy and so much less than the giver. It creates distance and ranking.

Gratitude in the Abundance model is a celebration of connect-edness and what we share. Gratitude builds intimacy and trust; it takes belonging for granted. All parties are honored and equal. The more fully we can receive and appreciate what is given to us, the more expansive we become. Our tolerance for bliss just keeps growing.

The future we create through the lens of Gratitude and mutuality is the route out of the Trance of Scarcity. Drinks are on the house!

9
Chapter

Generosity
and Giving

A wise woman was traveling in the mountains, when she came upon a beautiful, clear stream. Thirsty, she cupped her hand, reached in, and brought the water to her mouth. After she had drunk, she noticed a precious stone in the palm of her hand. She held it high and it glittered in the sun. Delighted, she tucked the treasure into her bag. The next day the wise woman met a hungry fellow traveler, and without hesitating she opened her bag to share what food she had. Immediately, the traveler caught sight of the precious stone and asked the woman to give it to him. She did so without the slightest hesitation.

The traveler left, rejoicing in his good fortune. This stone was surely worth enough money to provide a lifetime of security. But only a few days later, he came back, his brow furrowed, and returned the stone to the wise woman.

"I've been thinking," he said. "I know how valuable this stone must surely be, but I've brought it back to trade for something even more precious. Please give me what you have within you that enabled you to freely give me the stone."

Generosity:
Double Your Pleasure, Double Your Fun

Generosity closely follows the laws of physics. Each one of us is like a tub of water: Once you're full, you're definitely going to overflow! It would take much greater effort to try to contain it, to keep it in the tub, than to simply let it spill over and give itself to the floor. The wise woman in our story understood this. She also knew that when residing in fullness, you cannot be depleted.

Think of the generous people you know—if they have it, it's yours, too. They're the folks who are lavish hosts; neighbors who mow your lawn when you're busy; colleagues who help you prepare for a presentation for which you'll get all the credit; busy people who stop to give directions when you're lost. Generous people take pleasure in sharing what they have. It doesn't occur to them to dam up the flow, because they're too busy enjoying being *in* it. Generous people give because they know they have received. They don't identify with causing the flow to keep coming.

The origin of the word *generous* is linked to *magnanimous*, which in Latin means *great*. Makes sense, doesn't it? People who are generous are great, grand, and expansive, and it feels wonderful to be in their presence. Warren Bennis tells a story about Queen Elizabeth's two great prime ministers, William Gladstone and Benjamin Disraeli. Someone once observed that when you had dinner with Gladstone, you came away thinking that he was the wittiest, most intelligent, most charming person you had ever met. When you dined with Disraeli, he made you feel sure that *you* were the wittiest, most intelligent, most charming person ever.

. . . .

*Keep away from people who try to belittle your ambitions. Small
people always do that, but the really great make you feel that
you, too, can become great.*

Mark Twain

. . . .

When someone feels the freedom to let life, love, and plenty
flow without constriction, that freedom enables them to be truly
curious, interested in others, forgiving, and supportive. It is not
because they have a more noble character that people are generous—that's where we've gotten things twisted. Society has put
generosity on its righteous To Do list, right next to always being
on time and never questioning authority. Giving from a sense of
obligation takes all the fun out of it. Being Generous because you
"should" give takes it out of the realm of flow and into the realm of
rules, regulations, and judgment.

When you meet people who are not naturally generous, it
doesn't say a thing about their character. It tells you that they
are still caught in the Trance of Scarcity, still focused on getting
and keeping their share. Their orientation to life is that there isn't
enough to go around, and based on that reasoning they feel they
must hoard and stash. These people are like bugs on the inside
of a window screen. The bugs can see clearly that there is a vast
wonderland waiting out there, but they don't know how to be part
of it. Rather than venture toward vastness, many people choose to
stay safe—entranced and separate.

. . . .

We are what we repeatedly do.

Annie Dillard

. . . .

The Joyous Exhale

We're in the out-breath phase of our Cycle of Abundance now, which often feels every bit as nourishing and rewarding as the inhale. Openness followed by Fullness, followed by Openness, followed by Fullness. When we completely engage in both, we live in a state of wholeness. We cannot be diminished.

We may feel afraid when we extend, when we send out what is ours into the world. We may extend our genius, our love, our opinion, our cash, and sometimes it feels as though, now that we've sent it out, we will be forever separated from what we've given. Thank you, Trance of Scarcity, but no thanks! Nothing could be further from the truth. The wisdom shared by Fritjof Capra, Peter Senge, Margaret Wheatley, Ken Wilber, and other leaders empowers us to envision systems in their wholeness, rather than as merely a bunch of stuff that happens to be located in the same vicinity. Even our language works against our ability to see connectedness and interdependence. The word *wave* locks the water into a still snapshot, rather than identifying it as an endlessly rolling expression, indivisible from the ocean. Attempts to contain and label our experience often reduce our sense that we belong to the whole.

Neurochemistry now shows that when we are under stress, the brain's activity shifts down (toward the brain stem, which focuses solely on matters of survival) and loses its ability to make intelligent connections. If the brain remains overwhelmed—a chronic condition in our culture—it can't upshift to its higher functioning, in which it perceives patterns and wholeness. The Trance of Scarcity keeps the brain in perpetual downshift, where it's all about my own survival.

During Victoria's Adventures in Hell, my mind was riveted on survival issues much of the time. For six months I had been looking for work. This translated to 44 resumes sent out, 30 phone interviews, 19 preliminary in-person interviews, nine call-back interviews, five final interviews, and five of these: "Thank you, your credentials are very impressive, but we've chosen another candidate." I got really good wear out of my navy blue power suit. I sat in the plush offices of many organizations. I spoke to many nice people and a few odd ones. And to my way of thinking, I had the opportunity to say, "I appreciate your letting me know," about five times too many.

While all these conversations were doing wonders to grow my character, nothing was growing my bank account. The diminishing balance became increasingly frightening to behold. At last I was down to the double digits! I started putting only two dollars worth of gasoline into my car at a time, and parking several blocks from an interview rather than paying to park closer. Dinners at home were often brown rice with a little soy sauce (which is actually pretty good when you're hungry). I even washed my clothes by hand, rather than spend two-fifty at the laundromat. Out-of-town friends made a point of calling me so I wouldn't have to pay for long distance. Recreation consisted of walking to a fancy restaurant, waiting for the door to open, and catching a whiff of the great aromas wafting forth from within.

Then one day I heard about a lecture on prosperity, and I went. The speaker told her story of being left penniless in a foreign country by her husband. She went on to share how she had found her way out of that dire circumstance and learned the Laws of Prosperity. I was all ears.

She talked about Gratitude—check (I had just been to the Singles Group class and was doing my gratitude list every day). She mentioned a positive attitude—check. Being clear about what you want—check.

I was following right along until she said, "And be sure you are giving away some part of whatever you have, no matter how small the amount."

She couldn't have been talking to me, I thought. I mean, *my* little was really itty-bitty little. Timidly I raised my hand. "I only have $86 left and can't seem to find a job. Do you mean I should actually *give away* part of that?"

Her warm smile met me. "Wow, how exciting! Only $86! You get to jump right in and learn this quickly. Yes, I suggest you give away 10 percent of your $86. Give it to someone who has enriched your life. Oh, and be happy when you give it. Give it with an open heart."

At that moment I was vividly aware of my heart, because it was pounding in my throat. Meanwhile, my stomach was folding and refolding itself like origami. And my breathing . . . What breathing?

Then out of nowhere, a weird calm came over me and I got out my checkbook. "Oh, what's the worst that can happen?" I thought to myself. "It's summertime, after all. Being a bag lady won't be that bad." I wrote out a check, but not for a measly $8.60. I rounded it all the way up to $10. There was a basket by the door when the lecture was over, and people were invited to contribute. That was my cue.

As I left I put that check in the basket, and I actually felt happy about it. I was genuinely grateful for the speaker and her story, and also for her cheery confidence that I was going to be okay. I left with an open heart.

The next morning I awoke optimistic, ready for the tide to turn. The three companies I was currently pursuing had my resume in their hands and would surely be calling at any minute. I'll skip the waiting part of the story. They didn't call. But something else happened. A friend mentioned that a new restaurant had just opened and they were looking for experienced servers. I had spent much of my college life waiting tables. *I can do that with my eyes closed*, I thought.

For the next three months I went home with money in my hands every night, was able to pay my bills, slept soundly, and had my days free to look for "real" work. I was issued a uniform, got great meals for half price, and enjoyed socializing with my coworkers. It was no Cinderella story, but no bag lady story either. I waited tables only three months because by then I had landed a job in Seattle, hundreds of miles away. It was exactly what I had been looking for and meant I could return to the place I loved. I even met a guy with a van who was moving there too, and he hauled most of my things for no more than the cost of the gasoline. My financial picture rapidly improved, and so did my relationship with the flow—the constant flow of Abundance.

Since that time I have noticed something about people with plenty who enjoy giving and sharing what they have—they exude ease and relaxation. Worry is not their companion. They give constantly; it's simply what they do. The woman who spoke about the Law of Prosperity emanated just that level of ease. She knew without a shadow of a doubt that if I gave some of my money away, ease and flow would return to me, too.

Generosity   *Hoarding*

Who would have guessed that giving monetary gifts regularly will generate more money? How does that feel to you? For some, hearing this feels like the catch, the fine print. Others immediately agree it makes sense . . . in theory. Still others are already engaged in the practice of continual giving. A few don't even flinch because, just as I thought when I had only $86 left, they know this couldn't possibly apply to them because they don't have enough money for themselves, much less money to give away, for heaven's sake. They want to be generous, and they have plans to give just as soon as they have *enough*.

Reflect on the people who have made the biggest difference in your life: teachers, mentors, bosses, relatives, volunteers, authors, speakers, role models who have emboldened you to live out your greatness. Think of the folks who have seen who you are and called you forward, encouraged and invested in you, shared their genius openly and willingly with you. Has your world been expanded because of their offerings? What are the gifts you have received that keep enriching you, even now? Who are the people whose contribution to your life is so great that you could never repay it?

Take a moment and give yourself that lived experience of deep appreciation. Where do you feel that appreciation in your body? Can you let it well up in you, allow it to fill you? Give from that place. Remember that you are giving in response to having *already* received. You have taken in, and now you are like a tub of water that's overflowing. Spill and enjoy it!

Warning: Don't go near the slippery slope of "I *should* do this." Real Giving is not about *obligation* (which means *to constrain or bind*). Inspired Giving is at the opposite end of the map, in the land of plenty and ease and deep pleasure. Even if this sounds like what you've been instructed to do by parents or religious organizations, true Giving can only be done with joy. Forget trying to square your debt to the people who have given to you; you can never repay them, anyway. When you're truly Giving, you're not a consumer paying off what you owe. You're Giving because you want to open the gates even wider for good things to flow for your benefactors, for yourself, and for whoever comes after you.

. . . .

Joy is not incidental to your spiritual quest—it is vital.

Rabbi Nachman of Breslov

. . . .

Certainly, part of how you honor the gifts of your teachers and mentors is to become the best *you* that you can be, and then pass that on to others. The best you can be, of course, is whole, alive, and fully connected to your world. Inspired Giving is a practice that connects and relates us ever more deeply to whatever has inspired us in the past. Inspired Giving refills us again and again.

The dollar amount is up to you. There is no prescribed, correct amount. No inspired gift is too small. Each person discerns what is right for him. Often, the recipient is surprised and deeply touched. When you give, an important part of your gift is telling the person what she did, said, or offered that inspired you; it is important to deliver your appreciation as well as your gift. I still occasionally send a check with a note to teachers I studied with years ago, because the knowledge they entrusted to me keeps growing and maturing and I continue to be blessed by it. I don't ever want our interchange to stop.

. . . .

The true meaning of life is to plant trees under whose shade you do not expect to sit.

Nelson Henderson

. . . .

Once you engage in the practice of Inspired Giving, something else happens. You begin to notice all the ways in which inspiration comes to you. You actually become more inspired, and your field of vision opens up even wider. Great ideas appear, rich conversations present themselves, your timing seems to get better and better, traffic gets easier. It's as if the universe is conspiring on your behalf. And now you're awake to the fact. The more inspired you are, guess what? The brighter your energy, the bigger your contribution to the world and the greater your personal fulfillment.

If Inspired Giving is new to you, it can feel a little risky. Do it with intention, with a joyful heart. Like the wise woman in the story, you can never be diminished. If you feel a little edgy about money, you've got plenty of company. We live in a culture that encourages consuming and Hoarding. It perpetuates the state of scarcity, ever loyal to the Trance. Our two most precious commodities—time and money—are a good index for what really matters to us. We vote with our calendars and our checkbooks.

· · · · · · ·

Money is congealed energy (the ability to get things done).

Joseph Campbell

· · · · · · ·

Where do you want to get things done? Where do you want to spread a little energy? We live in a world in which money can make things happen. Money can be a positive force. In *The Soul of Money*, Lynne Twist writes, "Money becomes a conduit, a way to express our highest ideals. Money becomes the currency of love and commitment, expressing the best of who you are, rather than a currency of consumption driven by lack and emptiness."

Of course, we are by no means restricted to money as the only medium for giving. Because it is recognized internationally as a medium of exchange, a monetary gift is often the easiest to receive. We may give of our time, our goods, our creativity, our wit, our kindness. How the gift is used, how it is regarded, and whether it is shared remains at the discretion of the recipient. The great magic of giving money is that, given freely with intention, it can unite the material and spiritual aspects of our lives

The question is not *How much will I give?* but *What prevents me from giving?* What is it that keeps you from jumping into the pool and sharing the good, clean joy that is yours to share with everyone? The practice of true Giving increases your energy and well-being, and benefits the receiver. Heartfelt exchange, love, wonder, and appreciation all help to loosen the chronic contraction that so many of us hold in our bodies, our breath, and our being. The key is to let yourself be filled by what has been given to you, to expand into that fullness. From that fullness, Generosity happily spills out. The exhale just naturally follows the inhale.

Separate Tables

Wherever we perpetuate separation, we impoverish ourselves. Hoarding, the opposite of Generosity, banks on the notion that keeping everything we have for ourselves will assure our security. *If I can just stockpile enough of everything I will ever need,* we think, *I'll be secure. If I can keep from being contaminated, I'll be secure. If I can just not care too much, I'll be secure. If I can just get life to behave, I'll be secure.* Sadly, the strategy of self-insulation doesn't make us secure. Instead, it makes us indentured servants to insufficiency. The Trance of Scarcity strikes again!

When Tim and I were in the Santa Cruz earthquake in '89, all the stores in the area were closed because they were unsafe to enter. As we walked past Long's Drugstore, we saw a handwritten sign on the door that said "Please take what you need." Under the sign were 30 jugs of spring water and dozens of flashlights and batteries, just sitting there on the curb. We gratefully picked up a jug and a couple of batteries (we had our own flashlight) and started to walk on. Behind us, a fellow drove up in a sedan, opened the trunk, and proceeded to load *every single one* of the items on the curb into his car. We thought it might be the manager of the store, so we went back to thank him.

"Do you work here?" we asked.

"No," said the man, as he continued loading.

"Are you taking these to other people who don't have a car?"

"No."

"Oh, you're taking these for your family?"

"No, I'm not going to be inconvenienced. This is for me. Mind your own business."

Tim steered me away just as I opened my mouth, prepared to set the man straight about a few things.

I might have been annoyed with that man, but *he* was the one trapped in a cycle of suffering—he had accepted insufficiency as a way of life. Locked in the Trance of Scarcity, he couldn't afford to notice that there were other people in need all around him. He was utterly focused on *I-me-mine*. I didn't envy him.

. . . .

In a real sense all life is inter-related. All persons are caught in an inescapable network of mutuality, tied in a single garment of destiny. Whatever affects one directly, affects all indirectly. I can never be what I ought to be until you are what you ought to be, and you can never be what you ought to be until I am what I ought to be. This is the inter-related structure of our reality.

Martin Luther King, Jr.

. . . .

Maintaining our separation takes a lot of practice at squeezing down. What starts as a momentary reaction to our perceived lack soon becomes a way of life. Exclusion, chauvinism, and elitism are all forms of Hoarding: *This is mine, you people stay away*. Hoarding breeds callousness, a hardening of the heart that makes us impenetrable and unapproachable. Ironically, every action we take to protect ourselves, every choice that insists on *me first*, only reinforces our sense of insecurity and vulnerability.

No Martyrdom for Me, Thanks Anyway

Most of us were raised on the injunctions *Be good* and *Be good enough*. We were shown exemplary, saintly acts of good character so that the message came clear. In my upbringing, it meant that you should be kind, thoughtful, respectful, unselfish, and generous *until it hurt*. Martyrdom was honored, and with continued sacrifice, I, too, could achieve that status. Oh, the years of therapy it took to unwind that knot!

Historically, martyrs gave of themselves for a cause which cost them their lives. Pop psychology adopted the term *martyr* to refer to people who give in ways unhealthy both for themselves and for those around them. The image comes to mind of a stalwart woman biting her lip as she pulls the wagon without complaint, now that her husband has lost their horse in a poker game.

As we acclimate to the 21st century, it's clear that martyrdom simply will not fly. The age that idealized the roles of victim and hero is coming to an end, because both are inauthentic. They pale and wither beside the now-obvious truth of our interdependence. We're trading in victim/hero status for an upgrade: living with intention and power within the web of our connection to each other.

Acts of goodness take care of the giver as well as the receiver. Selfless service means being able to operate beyond your comfort zone. It does not mean pushing forward, giving recklessly while disregarding your needs and dreams. Generosity, at its healthiest and most rewarding, makes more room for all parties involved to live in their greatness.

PRACTICE
Generosity
• • • •

As a resident of the Circle, you can rest assured that all others belong even if they don't see it. I recommend a practice called *tonglen*, inspired by ancient Tibetan Buddhist meditation. This version is a simple and elegant way to join with others and to share your joy. The practice is done in the spirit of acknowledging that we are all connected, that we all share the experience of life.

1) Find three occasions each day when you feel full, blessed, joyful, or expanded, and take a moment to embrace the experience on behalf of all beings. The gift you embrace can be as simple as fresh air, good soup, or a full tank of gas.

2) Breathe in the richness of the moment, and breathe out the thought, "May everyone know _____ like this." You can fill in the blank with *peace, joy, ease, happiness, pleasure, nourishment, freedom, beauty, love*. You choose.

3) Feel your connectedness. Whatever affects one person directly, affects all of us indirectly. What happens for you when you freely share your bounty? Does your experience of Abundance diminish, or does it increase?

4) Do this practice anytime you notice a tendency to feel separate, insufficient, or shut down.

· · · · · · ·

*To get the full value of a joy, you must have someone
to divide it with.*

Mark Twain

· · · · · · ·

When someone dies, it's common to hear, "She lived a full life."
How do we measure the fullness of life? By how much we amassed,
how much we knew, how long we lived, how far we traveled, how
famous we were? Or do we measure it by how fully we experienced
the moments of life, our personal exchanges, our connections, our
sense of belonging? If we are inclined to hold on to what we have,
we choose a life that might at first glance appear more orderly,
but which is devoid of all the delicious, surprising messiness and
vibrancy of our humanity. The opposite of joy is not sadness, but
indifference. When we hold and grasp, we become indifferent.

How much indifference can your soul take before it begins to
wither? As a society, we seem to be exhibiting many of the traits of
the AIDS virus. The body turns on itself, destroying healthy cells,
rejecting anything that doesn't match the disease. Our attempt to
stay safe ends up robbing us of life.

· · · · · · ·

*We are not held back by the love we didn't receive in the past, but
by the love we're not extending in the present.*

Marianne Williamson

· · · · · · ·

If we open ourselves to feeling life beyond ourselves, must we
then pack up and move to Calcutta? That was Mother Teresa's calling; now you get to discover your own. To do this, listen for what
calls to you, what gets your attention, what you love, what you

want to be true. Then give to that calling in ways that excite you, stretch you, and embolden you. As you enter the flow, decide to be a paddle rather than a dam.

Giving: Nothing to Lose

The storage industry is one of the fastest growing in the U.S. economy. We seem to have an endless need to find more room for our stuff. How is it that our houses (on average now 30 percent larger than they were in the '60s) don't have enough room to store all the things we've accumulated? We rent space to house boxes of items which we never visit. If having and keeping are the name of the game, we're winning in a big way. But all this hoarding edges out the option of living in flow and of making room for what's next.

Giving is the delicious act of sending out what we value and releasing what burdens us. It is creative, spontaneous, invigorating, and natural to human beings to give and share. A tribal species, we're hardwired with certain desires. Among these are the need to be safe, to belong (or to be included), to be known, to be loved, and to contribute. The ability to contribute, to bring value, is a source of deep fulfillment. It's more than just seeking approval; it's knowing that our lives matter. If we cannot bear to give of ourselves or our possessions, we suffocate under the burden of accumulation.

· · · · · · ·

I have found that among other benefits,
giving liberates the soul of the giver.

Maya Angelou

· · · · · · ·

When I ask, "Why do you give?" the most common answer I hear is, "Because it feels good!" Giving carries within it the sense of completion, the exhale. If the lungs are full, taking in more is not possible or even desirable. Holding the breath quickly becomes uncomfortable; we can only sustain it for so long. Release—like breathing out when our lungs are filled—is the natural response to fullness. It's up to us to experience how much we already have, to acknowledge that we have already inhaled, so we can let go and exhale easily.

How we give reveals how we orient ourselves in the family of things. The movement that sparked the practice of Random Acts of Kindness (giving anonymously and in unexpected ways) became popular partly because it feels best to give without expectation of reward. Free from the need for applause or thanks, we simply enjoy the fun of unconditional giving. In my early 20s, I looked forward to Christmas as the season during which you could give unexpected gifts and do favors for people and get away with it. Then as I watched people keeping score about whom they owed for their gifts and how to repay them, my enthusiasm for the season faded.

There's no bartering in true Giving; it is an act complete in itself. The giver gives, and the receiver does whatever they do with what is given. They'll acknowledge it, appreciate it, use it, be enriched by it—or not. Clearly the less attached we are to how the recipient responds, the freer we are. Regardless of how appropriately the gift is received, the giving itself is complete.

In our zeal to give and contribute, we sometimes lose sight of how intrinsically related we all are. Father Anthony de Mello speaks of this beautifully. "Love springs from awareness," he writes. "When you set out to serve someone whom you have not taken the trouble to see, are you meeting that person's need or your own?" If giving is hooked to our identity, if we are giving because we want to see ourselves in a certain light, we do not see the recipient of our gift. This kind of giving is taking in disguise. We are giving on our own behalf, so that we can take away a high opinion of ourselves. Have you ever known someone with such a strong need to see himself as generous and supportive that he nearly smothered people in his fervor to attend to them? I can remember times when I have done exactly that. All my good intentions didn't amount to a hill of beans, because the intention underneath (unconscious though it may have been) was to get more esteem for myself.

Life Is Too Short to Wear Tight Shoes

Giving is pure, unbridled pleasure. Giving can be a truly voluptuous act. When you hold a door open for someone, offer directions to a tourist, prepare a meal for your guests, or articulate your appreciation for someone, do you feel more alive or less so? As we study the way to embody Abundance, our focus constantly returns to our capacity to allow more aliveness, and hence more pleasure, into our system.

Once we clearly understand that no matter what happens we cannot be diminished, we are truly free to give. This is the wisdom of the exhale: I can release all the air from my lungs with full confidence that a new, fresh breath of air will be there, just waiting for me to inhale. Not only am I not diminished by this letting go, I am enriched. What if our way of Giving was as easeful as releasing a relaxed, full breath of air? What might be possible then?

Take yourself back to the image of the Circle—the effortless, unimpeded flow. By consenting to be in the Circle, you consent to be part of the flow. Your belonging is a matter of consent rather than default because you (and only you) have the power to keep yourself out of the Circle. As I said before, the Latin root of the word *consent* is *consentire: to feel*. There's the aliveness factor again.

The more feeling, the more sensation and aliveness we allow

ourselves, the more present we are to life. The more present we are, the more we experience that we have a choice. We give out of choice, not out of obligation or restriction. Giving is not payment, and it's not business. Barter is a perfectly good form of exchange as long as it is recognized as such, as long as it doesn't masquerade as true Giving (without expectation of return). When we barter to belong, however, we pollute the flow.

. . . .

Life begets life. Energy creates energy. It is by spending oneself that one becomes rich.

Sarah Bernhardt

. . . .

As you build your capacity to allow aliveness to run freely within you, you are whole, regardless of what happens. From this experience of embodied wholeness, you need not spend one moment of attention defending or insulating yourself. The mere notion of stockpiling or limiting what flows out becomes completely unappealing, like the idea of eating a pizza right after a full meal: *Why would I do that to myself when I'm already full?* As you give up grasping and begin to follow the natural flow of life, you find happiness in what is.

There are thousands of ways to give. What is it that calls you? Action, kindness, wisdom, talent, money, time, connections, love, food, encouragement? The choice is yours. But be mindful: If you're not having a whopping good time of Giving, then stop. Check to be sure you are Giving from a sense of fullness, that you feel related, that you see to whom you are Giving, and that you haven't installed any dams in the flow. Check to see that you are still unattached to the results of your Giving. When all these are humming along, then once again you're free to radiate all over the place.

. . . .

Love isn't like a reservoir. You'll never drain it dry. It's much more like a natural spring. The longer and the farther it flows, the stronger and the deeper, and the clearer it becomes.

Eddie Cantor

. . . .

There is a simple and profound Zen teaching that encourages us to "keep the bowl empty." It invites us to rest in the impermanence of life rather than resist it. Things change, molecules move, doors open, people leave, ideas come, hearts open, bridges connect, peace returns. We do not reside in a static universe; we are free to release and open, moment to moment, for that which is waiting to arrive.

The Burden of Accumulation

Two hours in the company of lions—what could be better than that! I was thrilled on my way to attend a lecture by a naturalist who had spent months observing one pride of lions. He showed us his gloriously magnified slides on a six-by-eight-foot screen that brought us all directly into the experience.

The naturalist told us amazing stories with the pictures, about how the pride slept, ate, cleaned themselves, took care of their young, traveled to a new spot. We saw fascinating close-ups of the lions' paws, saw how they draped themselves over each other at rest and how they played with and disciplined the cubs. Our speaker had given them all names so he could refer to them easily. The male lion was Zeus; the three lionesses were Babette, Jeannette, and Lynette; the two cubs he had dubbed Spin and Marty.

Their names made them all the more charming.

How they got food was the most challenging to watch. One morning, Babette, Jeannette, and Lynette went stalking a small herd of zebras. As the herd broke and ran, one zebra lagged just far enough behind to become the focus of attack. In less than three minutes, the lionesses had identified, selected, and claimed their prey.

Quickly, Zeus and the cubs appeared. For the next two hours or so, the pride feasted on hide, flesh, bones, marrow, and organs. They ate with precision and gusto, their faces painted bright red with blood. Watching the slides, I could easily imagine the slurps and grunts of deep biological pleasure. The lions supped until they could stand to eat no more.

By now the sun was high in the sky, the heat intensifying as it met the ground. These cats with bulging bellies now had one agenda: find shade and sleep. They left the carcass in the sun and wandered to a spot about 100 yards away, where deep shade and comfort awaited.

Sleep came quickly for everyone except Babette. As the pride had moved further from its midday repast, she'd seen the jackals and vultures swoop in immediately to eat the leftovers. Babette turned back to them, roaring to send them away. But as soon as she settled back into the shade, the scavengers moved in again. The lioness returned to stand guard over the carcass. She watched the scavengers, satisfied that they would not come closer. As she watched her family members settling down for their naps, she clearly felt the longing to be resting beside them.

Babette moved toward the shade again, and once again the intruders came back. Again and again, she returned to the carcass while looking longingly at the pride. Then she had an idea. She would drag the carcass into the shady sleeping spot (the length of a football field). It didn't matter that the carcass no longer had any value for her. Full belly or no, that carcass belonged to her family and she wasn't sharing.

So Babette pulled. She sunk her teeth in, her muscles hunched and straining. The carcass moved a couple of inches. She strained again, and it budged another few inches. She glanced at the pride snoring in the cool shade, her eyes glazed over. She looked like someone who has had too much champagne at a summer wedding. She listed and then staggered, her body demanding to lie down and digest what she had already eaten. But the lioness remained determined to protect her spoils at all costs.

What to do, how to choose? It was a painful sight, each slide taking us deeper into the lioness's inner conflict. We viewed the slides for several minutes in silence, the story clear. As the lecturer clicked over to the next set of slides, he looked at the audience and said, "Just goes to show you . . . Don't let the things you own make you poor."

His words pinned me to my chair. It was 1975 and I was in love with a man who lived in another state. I had considered moving to be near him, but there I was, in my mid-20s, with the almost-perfect job, the totally perfect apartment, and all my dear friends close by. How could I leave all that, just for love? I walked into the winter night, pondering.

Certainly I wasn't letting the things I owned make me poor; not adventurous, independent me. I wouldn't let myself be defined by circumstances, would I?

By the time I drove home, I could see it. What I thought I had, actually had me! I called my long-distant love and the sound of his voice confirmed that I was ready to trade in my justification to stay put for the new possibilities that waited. I moved three months later, and within a year we married.

What are the thoughts, habits, and attachments that make you poor? Scan through your day, just today, for any places where you're stuck on holding and protecting, rather than allowing, opening, and flowing with the Cycle of Abundance. As long as you subjugate yourself to the Trance of Scarcity, you are doomed to repeat Babette's folly.

. . . .

He who obtains has little. He who scatters has much.

Lao Tzu

. . . .

The opposite of Giving is Stagnation, when we're plugged up and staying that way, when we've closed down and stopped Giving, holding on as though holding our breath: en-Tranced. Imagine a river with a dam at each end. Quickly the once-clear water becomes a muddy swamp, ideal for mosquitoes and sludge—not a likely setting for the flow of Abundance.

Giving   *Stagnation*

One of the ways we dam up the flow is by letting things linger and take up space in our lives. These clogging agents may be projects we will never complete, boxes we have yet to unpack from the last move, things we know we need to say but haven't yet mustered the courage to bring up, resentments toward ourselves or others. Such unfinished business is like a box of leftovers that's gone bad. Have you ever opened the vegetable drawer in your refrigerator and found a plastic bag of something green that had turned to liquid? That's what we're talking about. Something that's stinking up your place, stuff that's not worth keeping—no matter how much you paid for it.

To live with these incompletes requires going numb. The discomfort of seeing our unfinished business right under our nose every day is just too much, so to keep from feeling this discomfort, we keep adjusting our emotional rheostat lower and lower. Or we may torment ourselves repeatedly about how bad we are not to have addressed the issue, until we finally throw up our hands and admit to failure. While this tight armor may shield us from life's intensity, authors Joel and Michelle Levy say that "it also exhausts, depletes, and weakens us. Relaxation is a gesture of mercy, compassion, and kindness toward ourselves, and a step toward becoming more and more available to life, to trusting and embracing our wholeness."

PRACTICE
Giving
• • • •

Removing the encumbrances that make you poor is sweet liberation. Be gentle as you begin this process; to do it really well you need to be in the kind of mood that makes you want to clean out the refrigerator. Forcing yourself would be just another form of contraction. So pull on the rubber gloves of curiosity, and tie on the apron of wholeness. You may want to start with the smaller issues and gradually work up to the stickier ones.

1. Choose an issue that is damming the flow for you right now; it could be a tangible or an intangible barrier. It's always a good idea to look first in places where you're holding resentment or regret. Is there an unfinished project that looms over you? Are you willing to address it

now? If not, find one that you *are* ready to address.

2. Take time to open into the experience of fullness and wholeness. Allow your muscles to soften, your breath to grow wider. Enjoy your deepening connection to life as you replace contraction with flow. Linger here until you feel alive and connected. Notice how this shifts the way you're looking at your chosen issue.

3. Ask yourself: *Why is this issue important for me to release and complete? What will it take for me to do this?* Be realistic about how much time and energy the releasing and completion will take. Will you need support, perhaps a listener to hear the story you have to tell one last time? What will happen to your identity and capacity to engage with life if you address this unfinished business? What will happen if you don't address it?

4. Meet the issue as though it's a person sitting across from you. Tell it what you need it to know, either by speaking aloud or by writing a letter. Make the process as physical an act as is helpful. You might pull up an empty chair to have a conversation with your issue, or dig a hole to bury what is now finished. Or you might open a closet door and begin sorting. As you do your clearing, you might want to make a declaration: *I release my Story that you did me wrong and I am now finished holding a grudge* or *I choose not to spend any more time on you and I declare that I am not going to finish this project* or *I'm giving this away.* If you're clearing out a closet, pack up the stuff that needs to go and take it to a charity right away. Don't let that part of the process live as yet another To Do item. Complete it now.

5. Now put on some music you love, and sing and dance around the room! Call a friend and brag. Celebrate this

completion; don't treat it as a somber event. Reward yourself! You just reclaimed a part of your life force; enjoy it!

6. Ask your system—your breath, your muscles, your inner
   state—if it is ready for more releasing. If so, repeat the
   above steps. If not, make a promise to yourself about when
   you will check in again.

To truly give, and to experience the happiness and ease of flow,
we must know how to give to ourselves. Sometimes that gift is as
simple as emptying out the garbage. As long as we place conditions on our wholeness, our full experience of life, we are operating
under the rules of the Trance of Scarcity. Our wholeness is the
result of our state of being, and we have sovereignty there. Each
time we claim more aliveness, we embody more Abundance. This
is the way of wholeness.

We can gather a lot of evidence that we must keep scrambling
for survival, that we're always at the whim of circumstances. However, we can gather just as much evidence that our state determines
our course in life more than anything else, acknowledging that our
state is ours to direct. We choose which body of evidence serves
our purpose .

For most of us, our purpose is to live a rich, full, meaningful life.
We want to contribute in our own way, to do what is ours to do. My
dear friend, the late Danaan Parry, used to talk about the gift that is
unique to each one of us. We are each a steward for a piece of the
Great Wound and a piece of the Great Vision, he said. Our gifts
may feel very personal, but when each of us takes hold of our piece of
the great vision, nothing affirms our relatedness more readily.

We each have a wound that comes from our personal experience
of loss and separation, our sense of exile, and it helps to shape us.
Our vision is embedded within us, and shapes us as well. Our vision

is that insistent sense of the possible, the great view of what might be, regardless of current conditions. As we consciously step into the experience of the wound as well as the experience of the vision, the two are brought together in the heart. At that point alchemy takes place, creating the unique blend of wound and vision that is ours to bring into the world. The result is that earthly good is done through us, and we fulfill our purpose.

· · · · · · ·

If you ask me what I have come to do in this world, I will reply, I have come here to live aloud.

Emile Zola

· · · · · · ·

You have extraordinary gifts to bring into the world, and the world is counting on you to bring them. It's also counting on you to reside in the Circle rather than to stay in self-exile like too many others. The world needs you to release contraction a million times a day so that aliveness can flow freely in you, to not hold back who you are but give it freely. Let your connectedness to others inspire powerful, creative action. Be a living, flowing energy field of ease and belonging that cannot be denied.

We have traveled around the Cycle of Abundance, exploring the nature of flow and learning practices to merge with that flow in every moment. When we come to know that no matter what happens we cannot be diminished, we are enriched and empowered to remain open to every experience. We can let the flow move on without getting in its way. At this point in our journey, we become truly free from the dictates of circumstance. We become the embodiment of Abundance, living proof that the Trance of Scarcity is a Story that does not have the power to decide our destiny.

Chapter 10

Hello Abundance, Goodbye Trance!

I can't believe how I've exhausted myself by working on the wrong things!" Grant was delighted. After only two months as I coached him in practicees of embodiment, suddenly the light went on for him. Life no longer looked like one big problem after another. "Everything used to be so difficult. But it turns out I've been so tight and defended that I couldn't have felt any pleasure anyway, not even the pleasure that was already available. Being in the Circle is a lot more fun that staying out of it. Plus—now my life works!"

Grant quickly became the poster boy for Abundance. By loosening the chronic contraction he had held in his body for decades, by taking on a new state and a new *way of being*, he designed a different future to live into. Grant started his own business "where people are treated with the proper respect," healed a broken relationship with his son, and began hosting the annual block party in his neighborhood—all actions he would never have taken while living within the Trance of Scarcity. Once Grant had pierced the illusion of lack, separation, and struggle, he was able to put out the welcome mat for Abundance: living with ease and flow.

Everything that Grant had, you also have, right now. (*If you skipped to the last chapter to get a summary of the main points, welcome. It's the practices presented in this book that will lead you straight to embodiment, so don't settle for less.)* Here's a review of our all-star cast of state-changers and other actionable truths to help you Break the Trance and Embody Abundance.

• **Our experience of Abundance is determined far more by our inner state than by our outer circumstances.** The point of leverage for changing our circumstances is *how* we meet what happens to us, not changing the details of what's happening. We humans are meaning-makers—we decide what something means to us. Out of our assigned meaning grow all our choices and actions. And the meaning we assign is entirely based on our inner state.

• **Our state is the product of our Soma (how we Inhabit ourselves) and our Story (how we Orient ourselves).** We are complex, multi-dimensional psychobiological beings, not machines.

Soma ~ How we Inhabit ourselves. Do we contract, or open to the breath and aliveness in our system? How do we shape ourselves, and how do we move under pressure? How do we occupy our space? All these produce a certain Soma. The more frozen, clenched, braced, and tense we are, the more scarcity we experience in our lives. The more fluid, relaxed, curious, and available to the present moment we are, the more we experience the flow of Abundance.

Story ~ How we Orient ourselves. How do we interpret ourselves, others, and life in general? What meaning do we assign to what happens throughout the day? What is the filter or mood that we are peering through? How do we decide whether we belong in the Circle or should be exiled from it? All these produce a certain Story. A Story can never be true—after all, it's just something we made up. But rather than picking a Story that stifles us, we can choose a Story that is useful given what matters to us.

• **The same ingredients that produce our state—Story and Soma—also produce our reality.** Because they create our reality, by shifting them we can shift our reality into a more pleasurable mode. To do this, we must engage the power of both Story and Soma. It's not magic. It's simply a matter of using the ingredients that will produce true and lasting results.

· · · · · · ·

The greatest thing in education is to make the nervous system our ally instead of our enemy.

William James

· · · · · · ·

• **When we expose the Trance of Scarcity for what it is—an unexamined Story (not the Truth)—suddenly it loses its grip on our lives. We are then free to create new ways of being that align us with ease and flow.** Under the Trance of Scarcity, the best we can hope to do is to continue refining our strategy for surviving inside the Story of our *not-enough-ness*. Recognizing that this is a Story and not the truth is the first step to living a new reality, both personally and globally. The more disembodied we are, the more susceptible we are to the Story of the Trance, and the more we take on that contracted Soma.

You may ask, "But isn't that a callous view? What about all the people in this world who are living in horrific conditions? Are you saying that their situation is their own fault?" It's a valid question, and it brings us to the heart of the matter of what it means to embody Abundance in the world. Out of our deep desire to change the poverty and suffering that exists, I suggest that we pose this question: **What if our global Story of scarcity (along with the poverty and miserable living conditions that exist in so many parts of the world) is not the *result* of world events and circumstances, but the *source* of those events and circumstances?** How might the world situation shift if we rewrote the Story?

• **Human nature is changeable, not static.** As long as we have a pulse, we are malleable. No matter how stuck we may feel, the essential elements (Story and Soma) are available to us. Once we understand how to put Story and Soma to proper use, we have the power to create a new experience of life.

*What we practice, we become.** If we want a new experience, we take on the practices that allow us to embody a different Story. Recurrent practice is our strongest ally for accomplishing permanent, positive change. True embodiment is the result of recurrent practice over an extended period of time. Practice isn't a job; it's what we naturally do. We are always practicing *something*. The question is, does our practice support what matters to us?

• **The Cycle of Abundance naturally replenishes itself.** When we actively engage in the practices of the Cycle, we free ourselves from the grip of the Trance of Scarcity. We begin to embody the state of ease and flow. Once we fully embody the easeful state of flow, we cannot be depleted.

In **Aligning**, we give up forcing life to turn out well, and open ourselves up to inspiration.

In **Attracting**, we give up grasping and straining from a place of doubt, and focus our attention on confident expectation.

In **Receiving**, we give up numbing ourselves, and become permeable to all that comes to us, so that we are filled.

In **Gratitude**, we give up the arrogance that kept us distant and dissatisfied, and deepen our pleasure and connection to life.

In **Generosity**, we give up hoarding and the constant push for more, and happily experience spilling over and wanting others to have what we have.

In **Giving**, we give up stagnation in which we're held captive by what we have, and we send out and release, making room for whatever comes next.

• **Pleasure is a powerful way to wake up to Abundance**. The Trance of Scarcity keeps us asleep, tightened up, closed down. Pleasure is the pure antidote. As soon as we open up to the pleasure of this present moment, we shift our state to allow for fresh, new possibilities. Our only task is to allow more life to move through the system.

• **All of life is interconnected; therefore, we all belong.** It is impossible to extract ourselves from the web of life. Even if we temporarily pull ourselves out of the Circle, our place is always reserved, waiting for us. No one is excluded from the Circle.

·······

Everyone has the longing to feel the open heart, because it is a deep happiness that can never be taken away.

Pema Chödron

·······

The Time Is Now, the Place Is Here

Imagine that you and ten of your closest friends embody Abundance so fully that it your default *way of being* in the world. How does that change your experience of life? Imagine that your children's teachers all embodied Abundance. Or the owners of your favorite businesses. Or the executives who run hospitals and insurance companies. Imagine that the leaders of nations made decisions and set policies based on the Story of Abundance rather than the Trance of Scarcity. Would you enjoy living in that world? Gandhi said, "Be the change you wish to see in the world." For most of us, "being the change" involves a bit (or a lot) of personal development. That's what we have been addressing throughout this book—how to embody Abundance as our natural *way of being* in the world. It won't help to deny the reality of scarcity; such struggle only creates more struggle. Instead, we've been experimenting with stepping outside of a Story that doesn't serve our future. To the extent that we're caught up in deciding who will get their needs met and who won't, we're still operating inside the Trance. If we're working from inside the Trance, any solution we find will only perpetuate the state of lack, separation, and struggle.

. . . .

Ethics is how we behave when we decide we belong together.

Brother David Steindl-Rast

. . . .

We influence each other whether we mean to or not. My mother loved me and I'm sure she wanted only to have the best influence on me that was possible. But when she told me at age seven that "people don't like little girls who are loud," the message shaped my behavior for the next 30 years. When Tim and I were in the Santa Cruz earthquake and Long's Drugstore put out free water and flashlights for anyone who needed them, instantly I became their loyal customer even though I had never been inside Long's before. When people grow up hearing that they are the victims of circumstance, they brace themselves to lead small and powerless lives.

Quantum physics has proven that we have a definite impact on everything around us. If the world is indeed created particle by particle, it is certainly not finite and unchangeable. Perhaps our role is to influence where even one of those particles resides—whether inside or outside the Circle. As we noticed earlier when we stepped into the Cycle of Abundance, when we are full we can't help overflowing. When you find a great restaurant or movie or book, you want to share it with all your friends. It's the natural exhale after the natural inhale—the release that follows the intake. This process takes nothing at all away from you. You are never diminished by sharing; in fact, the opposite is often the case. The more you spread the wealth, the wealthier and more abundant you feel and are. If you know how to embody Abundance, it's impossible not to want the same thing for everyone else.

Even if you would really rather not consider another person, if you'd prefer just focusing on yourself, it's too late for that. In fact, it's always been too late for that. Your innate sense of caring has eliminated any chance of your remaining callous and untouchable. If your aim was truly to squeeze down tighter and to keep life out, you would never have picked up this book and started reading. The reason that so many of us avoid watching or reading the news is not because we don't care, it's because we feel overwhelmed by the issues and our seeming inadequacy to address them.

· · · · · · ·

*How do we rediscover our innate capacity to connect
on behalf of our shared future?*

Peter Senge

· · · · · · ·

In the 1970s, employees of the newly founded Environmental Protection Agency wore a button that said, "Does it have to be this way?" I remember how much I wanted one of those, but no one would part with theirs. Everyone wore the button proudly. Part of the early work of the EPA was to call attention to potential environmental hazards and to invite innovative solutions. The EPA legitimized the question, "Do we have a choice about how we are operating? Are there other options available to us?" Right now, every one of us is living within that question on a daily basis.

In his bestselling book *Collapse*, Jared Diamond asserts that the real issues are not things we are powerless to change—like asteroids speeding toward planet Earth. Rather, "our biggest problems are the ones we are generating ourselves." Whatever we generate is the result of our perception, which, in turn, is the result of our state, which is the result of our Story and Soma. We're back to square one: the elements that create our reality. If we want to intervene in solutions to our biggest problems, we must address them at the level of cause rather than address their symptoms after the fact. The Trance of Scarcity will always keep us trapped inside a certain way of thinking, a certain embodiment, a certain state, Soma, and Story—which, by its very nature, prevents arriving at real solutions. As we all bear witness to the condition of humankind and our global environment, our greatest need is for people who are willing to step into the Circle and think outside the Trance.

Shadow Boxing

When I was 10 years old, my parents would go across the street to play cards at the neighbors' house, leaving me and my 12-year-old brother at home. Usually our way of misbehaving was to watch TV and ignore our homework, but on particularly dark and stormy nights, my brother engaged in his favorite form of entertainment— terrorizing his sister.

My brother would pretend to be really scared. Trembling, he would ask me whether I, too, saw the Stickman outside the window. He'd cower at the window and whisper to me, "Did you see him, he's really close! Look—he's coming closer! I think there may be more than one of them . . . You'd better go look!"

Terrified, I would creep to the window that looked out on our backyard, edging my eyes just far enough past the doorframe to see outside.

"He's right there—*look out!*" my brother would scream over my shoulder as he ran out of the room. The perfect patsy, I would race after him, believing that my brother was my only hope of safety in the face of the Stickman.

We would go through a few rounds of this until I couldn't take it anymore and approached the phone to call my parents. "Oh no, that's okay Sis. Look, he's gone now," my brother would quickly reassure me. Then he would smugly resume watching TV while I kept one watchful eye on the backyard.

It was years before I realized how that dastardly trick worked: my brother turned on the outside light to cast ominous shadows throughout the yard. He used his knowledge of light and shadow to torment me for more years than I care to admit. Without that light to cast a creepy shadow, there would have been no illusion of a lurking Stickman.

Now that I'm grown, I'm much wiser about shadows. Not only are they not to be feared, but you can walk right through them. They have no substance in themselves. The existence of a shadow depends solely on how the light is cast.

Illusions, like shadows, scared my 10-year-old self so much that I wouldn't walk into my own backyard. What I believed to be true determined what I did and did not do; I never thought beyond it. I created that reality based on a misinterpretation of the play of light and shadow. Now I know to pay closer attention to the source of the light.

· · · · · · ·

All change results from a change in meaning.

Margaret Wheatley

· · · · · · ·

Waking Up to Abundance:
A Radical Act

Pioneers and explorers have a lot in common. Considered fools by some and champions by others, either way they mess with our reality. When we're stuck in a downward cycle, though, having our reality messed with can be a good thing. That's often when we're most willing to entertain new interpretations. Our energy moves away from defending what's already in place—the status quo—to exploring what might be possible.

Thomas Berry, a cultural historian who has studied and written extensively about ecological issues, writes that each generation or historical age has a particular task that it must accomplish. It is not a task of our choosing, but a role given to us. "The nobility of our lives," says Berry, "depends upon the manner in which we come to understand and fulfill our assigned role."

Could it be that the task of our moment in history is to pierce the oppressive veil of the Trance of Scarcity—to discover a more robust way to engage in life? It may seem that our generation already has an overwhelming laundry list of tasks to accomplish and problems to solve. But what if addressing this *one crippling delusion* gave us access to the new way of thinking that could solve a whole array of humanity's current challenges? It would be like winning the lottery. What would happen if we infused the cultural conversation with a new distinction called the Trance of Scarcity?

In studying the nature of change in her book *Finding Our Way*, Margaret Wheatley observes that "both individual and organizational change starts from the same need: the need to discover what's meaningful." It isn't about making anyone wrong for their beliefs, nor is it about trying to convert others. Real change occurs by inviting people into the most compelling and vital conversation they can imagine, the one they hunger for. The more inclusive the conversation, the richer the results and the more invigorated and revitalized the participants. As Margaret observes, meaning behaves like energy. "Meaningful information lights up a network and moves through it like a windswept brush fire." It doesn't take an enormous amount of work to make such a conversation grow. Just make it meaningful, and watch it travel.

· · · · · · ·

Despair is cheap. Anyone can do that on their own. Hope is a thing you generate in yourself by recognizing that despair is a luxury. . . . Since most of us aren't burdened by terrible circumstances, we have an ethical obligation to look for hope and to find it.

Tony Kushner

· · · · · · ·

In a culture that reinforces contraction as the preferred means for getting through the day, resignation and despair come easily to most of us. *It's too much!* we exclaim. *I'm just one person. You can't beat the system.* And in one sense, it's true. If we play the game of exclusion rather than accept that we all belong, everything becomes too much and we feel inadequate to rise to the occasion. In the absence of a compelling purpose, we fall prey to operating in the victim mode where all power lies outside of us. The precious elixir is *connection*. Together we shift the prevailing conversation away from *why it can't work* and place our focus on *how it can succeed*. As Peter Block, author and consultant extraordinaire, asserts, "The answer to *How?* is *Yes!*"

Ambassadors of Abundance

When you think about it, how many times can you visit your own personal website to read your latest lengthy blog on "How I'm feeling about life today" before you yearn for something a little more meaty? More and more, my clients are becoming focused on the positive impact they can make, the legacy they will leave behind—that's where life feels juiciest for them. They have found that the most appealing game we human beings get to play consists of making our own unique contribution. Why not be a full player? Why not rush the field with absolute gusto and determination? The cure for the tedium of narcissism is big-picture consciousness. Taking the global view also erases the old sense of isolation or exclusion, of being outside the Circle. If you want to experience that healthy jolt of self-worth, it's time to suit up!

We all know people who quietly go about making their contributions. I think of my neighbor Hank, who works full-time and has a family, yet regularly checks in with all the older people in our neighborhood for any repairs or errands they might need done. There's my client Dennis who, seeing the challenge his employees had in finding affordable childcare, collaborated with the local community college to start a program that provided childcare on-site at his business, staffed with Child Development students earning academic credit while working under supervision. There's my friend Anne who, in her 70s, is so busy mentoring young women business leaders that she doesn't have time to age. Or my friend Staci, who started an organization to end the sexual abuse of children and, knowing full well that the work would not be completed in her lifetime, named it Generation Five in anticipation of effecting the change within five generations. Such people are not always those with extra time on their hands, but they jump in with whatever they have to give—at first sometimes simply vision plus willingness. By engaging fully in the flow and joyfully bringing what is theirs to bring, they give themselves to life, and life gives its best to them.

There are individuals and organizations everywhere who operate within the Cycle of Abundance. Their work is inspired and generative. One of my role models is Mohammed Junus, founder of the **Grameen Bank in Bangladesh** and the pioneer of micro-lending to the poor. Though again and again he received no cooperation from banks, he refused to accept the Story that the poor are not credit-worthy. He went on to loan (and to be repaid) millions of dollars, while transforming lives as people moved from poverty to self-sufficiency. He changed the prevailing reality by questioning its underlying Story—an assumption that had lived in people's minds so long it seemed like the truth.

Many other organizations have insisted on a different conversation around scarcity and abundance. **ONE, The Campaign to Make Poverty History** addresses global AIDS and extreme poverty, and reminds us that every one of us can make a difference.

You may have seen the organization's white bracelet on the wrists of countless celebrities. Through a diverse coalition of faith-based and anti-poverty organizers, the campaign attends to the shared future of all, fostering collaboration between wealthy nations and the countries most burdened.

Heifer International works to end hunger while caring for the earth. There, your donation buys an animal that will be provided to a family, granting them both food to eat and a means to make a living. Recipients agree to share the offspring of their gift animals with others in need, making them equal partners with Heifer in replacing hunger with sustainability.

The Pachamama Alliance works to empower indigenous peoples to preserve their territories and ways of life. Pachamama accomplishes its work not by intruding and instructing those peoples, but by partnering and learning with them and from them for the sake of a global vision of equity and sustainability for all. Pachamama's guiding vision is that indigenous cultures, if allowed to thrive, can teach us volumes about living in the lap of Abundance.

Riane Eisler, author of the groundbreaking *The Chalice and the Blade* and *The Power of Partnership*, has started **The Alliance for a Caring Economy**. The initiative calls upon government, academia, business, and civil society to recognize and reward the value of the essential work of caring for children and the elderly, keeping our families healthy, and maintaining a clean and healthy environment—the very elements traditionally overlooked by large corporations and conglomerates. The initiative resists the notion that some roles are simply insignificant, and that someone must always end up on the short end of the stick. The Alliance is redefining the configuration of the stick so that there is no short end.

The Berkana Institute, a global charitable foundation, serves and links life-affirming leaders in many countries. Margaret Wheatley, president of the Institute, has a firm resolve to find ways to lead and organize that affirm rather than destroy life. The Institute defines a leader as "anyone who wants to help," and provides a means for ordinary citizens to step up and do just that.

A free website, **www.gratefulness.org**, is the inspiration of **A Network for Grateful Living** (ANGeL), a nonprofit organization led by Brother David Steindl-Rast and others who envision a worldwide community whose members relate to one another in the spirit of an all-embracing family. You can visit the website to read articles, light a virtual candle, find practices, and make a donation. To practice gratitude is to deepen our mutuality and embrace our connection.

Happily, I could go on and on. That's the good news. These are just a few examples of individuals and organizations sponsoring compelling, meaningful conversations intended to foster an Abundant world Story. These folks do not practice domination, restriction, or exclusion, and they prosper. They are not blinded by the Trance of Scarcity's insistence that lack, separation, and struggle are our only reality, the one we must pass on to our children. Instead, parting company with the Trance, they are rewriting the governing Story of our time: We all belong, and together we can create a new reality—beginning with our own.

•••••••

True happiness, we are told, consists of getting out of one's self;
but the point is not only to get out—you must stay out, you
must have some absorbing errand.

Henry James

•••••••

Have a Great Life, Please

The fuller, richer, and more meaningful your life is, the better it is for everyone around you. So as we contemplate our shared future, I'll leave you with a simple assignment: Embody Abundance. Live in the world with ease. The very fact that you embrace life heightens your vitality, your resourcefulness, your resilience, your connectedness, and ultimately your contribution to the world. Since you won't be wasting a moment of your time mired in struggle and sacrifice, you'll have all that energy available to do something. Why not spread it around and enjoy every minute of it!

Here's what you can do:

- Embody Abundance as a *way of being*.
- Invite those around you into a conversation about what really matters to them.
- Ask "Why not?" whenever you encounter an unquestioned decree of *not-enough-ness*.
- Listen for when others are trapped in their own version of the Trance of Scarcity, and offer, with great respect and compassion, a different interpretation or two (or ten).
- Gather a half dozen friends and take on the practices in this book as a study group over the next 12 weeks. Make it fun!
- Let yourself reflect on what matters to you, on what you most want for this world. Then find a way to take action that supports that. If you find an organization that is already doing something about your particular concern, ensure that their strategies are based in Abundance and not trapped inside the Trance of Scarcity. Stretch the thinking around you.
- Live your life like one ongoing, voluptuous experience. Stay open and available to all the gifts flowing your way. Receive fully. Live

your rich and meaningful life without apology; be an invitation to others to step up to the buffet.

• Find a way to express your love every day, whether up close and personal, or anonymously. Keep those pipes clean, communicate clearly. Don't let stuff back up.

• Never for one moment entertain the thought that you don't matter. You most definitely do!

. . . .

If we choose to do so, we can turn the Trance of Scarcity into a teaching Story that will be used by future generations to explain how Stories can control our lives even on a planetary level. We can issue a warning that shows how, unless we remain aware of Stories as what they are—just Stories and nothing more—they can take on the appearance and power of the Truth. We can introduce a new competence to our children, colleagues, neighbors, and friends so they won't be fooled by Stories. Doing this, we can end the tyranny of unexamined Stories.

When Abundance becomes embodied—when it lives in you as a *way of being*, you move with great ease. You are propelled through life by clarity and purpose. Your wholeness is undeniable, irresistible; and it becomes a map that shows the way for others. When you embody Abundance—in your cells, in your breath, in your walk, in your way of thinking and feeling and celebrating—you can't help but serve those around you. A world in which you have more to give than you can possibly enjoy by yourself, in which you spend your joyful days constantly offering your unique contribution and watching the benefits accrue . . . now that's paradise. And what do you know? There's plenty of room for us all.

Bibliography

Bennis, Warren. *Managing the Dream: Reflections on Leadership and Change.* Cambridge, Mass.: Perseus Books, 2000.

Berry, Thomas. *The Great Work: Our Way into the Future.* New York: Harmony/Bell Tower, 1999.

Bohm, David. *Thought As a System.* New York: Routledge, 1994.

Buber, Martin. *I and Thou.* Free Press, 1971.

Campbell, Joseph. *The Power of Myth.* New York: Doubleday, 1988.

Capra, Fritjof. *The Hidden Connections: Integrating The Biological, Cognitive, and Social Dimensions of Life into a Science of Sustainability.* New York: Doubleday, 2002.

————*The Web of Life: A New Scientific Understanding of Living Systems.* New York: Anchor, 1996.

Chödron, Pema. *Comfortable with Uncertainty: 108 Teachings on Cultivating Fearlessness and Compassion.* Boston: Shambhala, 2003.

————*When Things Fall Apart: Heart Advice for Difficult Times.* Boston: Shambhala, 2000.

Csikzentmihalyi, Mihaly. *Creativity: Flow and the Psychology of Discovery and Invention.* New York: HarperCollins, 1996.

————*Flow: The Psychology of Optimal Experience.* New York: Harper & Row, 1990.

Damasio, Antonio. *Descartes' Error: Emotion, Reason, and the Human Brain.* New York: G.P. Putnam, 1994.

deMello, Anthony. *Wellsprings.* Image, 1986.

Diamond, Jared. *Collapse: How Societies Choose to Fail or Succeed.* New York: Viking, 2004.

Dominguez, Joe, and Vicki Robin. *Your Money or Your Life: Transforming Your Relationship With Money and Achieving Financial Independence.* New York: Viking, 1992.

Eisler, Riane. *The Power of Partnership: Seven Relationships That Will Change Your Life*. Novato, Calif.: New World Library, 2002.

Elgin, Duane. *Voluntary Simplicity: Toward a Way of Life That Is Outwardly Simple, Inwardly Rich*. New York: Quill, 1993.

Emoto, Masaru. *The Hidden Messages in Water*. Hillsboro, Ore.: Beyond Words Publishing, 2004.

Epstein, Mark. *Going to Pieces without Falling Apart*. New York: Broadway Books, 1998.

Fritz, Robert. *Path of Least Resistance: Learning to Become the Creative Force in Your Own Life*. New York: Ballantine Books, 1989.

Fuller, R. Buckminster. *Critical Path*. New York: St. Martin's Press, 1981.

Gladwell, Malcolm. *Blink: The Power of Thinking Without Thinking*. New York: Little, Brown, 2005.

Goswami, Amit. *The Self-Aware Universe: How Consciousness Creates the Material World*. New York: Putnam, 1993.

Harrington, Anne. *The Placebo Effect: An Interdisciplinary Exploration*. Cambridge, Mass.: Harvard University Press, 1999

Hawkins, David. *Power vs Force: The Hidden Determinants of Human Behavior*. Carlsbad, Calif.: Hay House, 2002.

Houston, Jean. *The Search for the Beloved: Journeys in Sacred Psychology*. New York: J. P. Tarcher, 1987.

Jamison, Kay Redfield. *Exuberance: The Passion for Life*. New York: Knopf, 2004.

Johnson, Don. *Body, Spirit, and Democracy*. Berkeley, Calif.: North Atlantic Books, 1994.

Keleman, Stanley. *Somatic Reality*. Berkeley, Calif.: Center Press, 1982.

King, Serge Kahili. *Urban Shaman*. New York: New York: Fireside, 1990.

Lamott, Anne. *Bird by Bird: Some Instructions on Writing and Life*. New York: Pantheon, 1994.

Leonard, George. *Mastery: The Keys to Success and Long-Term Fulfillment*. Plume Books, 1992

Leonard, George, and Michael Murphy. *The Life We Are Given*. New York: J. P. Tarcher, 1995

Levey, Joel and Michelle. *Living in Balance: A Dynamic Approach for Creating Harmony & Wholeness in a Chaotic World*. Berkeley, Calif.: Conari Press, 1998.

Lewis, Thomas, Fari Amini, Richard Lannon. *A General Theory of Love*. New York: Random House, 2000.

Lietaer, Bernard. *The Future of Money*. London: Random House, 2001.

Lipton, Bruce. *The Biology Of Belief: Unleashing The Power Of Consciousness, Matter And Miracles*. Memphis: Mountain of Love, 2005

Maslow, Abraham. *Toward a Psychology of Being*. New York: Van Nostrand Reinhold, 1982.

Maturana, Humberto. *Tree of Knowledge*. Boston: Shambhala, 1992.

Murray, W. H. *The Scottish Himalaya Expedition*. London: Dent, 1951.

Palmer, Wendy. *Intuitive Body: Aikido As a Clairsentient Practice*. Berkeley, Calif.: North Atlantic Books, 2000.

Parry, Danaan. *Warriors of the Heart*. Santa Fe, N.M.: Sunstone Press, 1991.

Pelletier, Kenneth. *Sound Mind, Sound Body: A New Model For Lifelong Health*. New York: Fireside, 1995.

Perls, Frederick. *Gestalt Therapy Verbatim*. Lafayette, Calif.: Real People Press, 1969.

Ray, Paul, and Sherry Anderson. *The Cultural Creatives: How 50 Million People Are Changing the World*. New York: Harmony Books, 2000.

Richards, Robert J. *Darwin and the Emergence of Evolutionary Theories of Mind and Behavior*. Chicago: University of Chicago Press, 1989.

Rubenfeld, Ilana. *The Listening Hand: Self-Healing Through The Rubenfeld Synergy Method of Talk and Touch*. New York: Bantam, 2000.

Salk, Jonas. *Anatomy of Reality: Merging of Intuition and Reason*. New York: Columbia University Press, 1983.

Schaef, Anne Wilson. *When Society Becomes an Addict*. San Francisco: HarperSanFrancisco, 1988.

Senge, Peter. *Presence: Human Purpose and the Field of the Future*. Cambridge, Mass.: Society for Organizational Learning, 2004.

Sheldrake, Rupert. *The Presence of the Past: Morphic Resonance and the Habits of Nature*. Rochester, Vt.: Park Street Press, 1995.

Steindl-Rast, David. *Gratefulness, The Heart of Prayer: An Approach to Life in Fullness*. New York: Paulist Press, 1984.

Stern, Daniel. *The Interpersonal World of the Infant: A View from Psychoanalysis and Developmental Psychology*. New York: Basic Books, 2000.

Strozzi-Heckler, Richard. *The Anatomy of Change: A Way to Move Through Life's Transition*. Berkeley, Calif.: North Atlantic Books, 2003.

————*Being Human At Work: Bringing Somatic Intelligence Into Your Professional Life*. Berkeley, Calif.: North Atlantic Books, 1993.

————*Holding the Center: Sanctuary in a Time of Confusion*. Berkeley, Calif.: Frog, Ltd., 1997.

Swimme, Brian. *The Universe Is a Green Dragon: A Cosmic Creation Story*. Rochester, Vt.: Bear & Company, 1984.

Tart, Charles. *Open Mind, Discriminating Mind: Reflections on Human Possibilities*. New York: Harper & Row, 1989.

Tutu, Desmond. *No Future Without Forgiveness*. New York: Doubleday, 1999.

Twist, Lynne. *The Soul of Money: Transforming Your Relationship with Money and Life*. New York: W. W. Norton & Company, 2003.

Van Doren, Charles. *A History of Knowledge: Past, Present, and Future*. New York: Ballantine, 1992.

Walcott, Derek. *Collected Poems, 1948-1984*. New York: Farrar, Straus and Giroux, 1987.

Wells, Rebecca. *Divine Secrets of the Ya-Ya Sisterhood*. New York: HarperCollins, 1996.

Wheatley, Margaret. *Finding Our Way: Leadership for an Uncertain Time*. San Francisco: Berrett-Koehler Publishers, 2005.

————*Leadership and the New Science: Discovering Order in a Chaotic World*. San Francisco: Berrett-Koehler Publishers, 1999.

Whybrow, Peter. *American Mania: When More Is Not Enough*. New York: W. W. Norton & Company, 2005.

Wilber, Ken. *A Brief History of Everything*. Boston: Shambhala, 2001.

————*Boomeritis: A Novel That Will Set You Free!* Boston: Shambhala, 2003.

Winograd, Terry, and Fernando Flores. *Understanding Computers and Cognition: A New Foundation for Design*. Boston: Addison-Wesley, 1987.

Index

To schedule seminars, retreats,
and keynote presentations
with Victoria Castle, please call
1-877-689-2800
or go to
www.TranceofScarcity.com

Possible topics:
1) Living into Greatness
2) Embodied Abundance
3) Trance-free Organizations
4) Generating a Culture of Abundance
5) Breaking the Trance in Body, Mind, and Spirit
6) Detecting the Trance in Action

Victoria Castle
c/o Sagacious Press
P.O. Box 1001
Clinton, WA 98236

ORDER FORM

The Trance of Scarcity

Victoria Castle

TITLE	US	CDN	QTY
The Trance of Scarcity	$15.97 / $19.66		

Shipping & Handling add $4.95 US _____

Sales Tax (WA State residents only, add 8.9%) _____

Total Enclosed _____

_____

Name _____

Address_____

City_____ State_____ Zip_____

Phone (   ) _____ Fax (   ) _____

Method of Payment:

__ VISA   __ MasterCard   __ Check or money order enclosed
made payable to Sagacious Press

_____ ____/____

Card number   Exp. Date

_____

Signature

Order by Mail: Order by Phone:
Sagacious Press   Call 1-877-689-2800
PO Box 1001
Clinton, WA 98236

Order autographed copies online at: **www.TranceofScarcity.com**
Quantity discounts available.

For more information, e-mail **info@TranceofScarcity.com**